THE WORLD'S REFUGEES
A Test of Humanity

THE WORLD'S

Refugees

A Test of Humanity

BY GIL LOESCHER WITH ANN DULL LOESCHER

ILLUSTRATED WITH PHOTOGRAPHS

HARCOURT BRACE JOVANOVICH, PUBLISHERS   HBJ
SAN DIEGO   NEW YORK   LONDON

ACKNOWLEDGMENTS: The authors and publisher wish to express their appreciation for permission to reprint the material that appears on the following pages of this book: Pages 2 to 8, from *American Mosaic: The Immigrant Experience in the Words of Those Who Lived It,* by Joan Morrison and Charlotte Fox Zabusky. Copyright © 1980 by Joan Morrison and Charlotte Fox Zabusky. Reprinted by permission of the publisher, E. P. Dutton, Inc.; pages 10–12, from *We Came as Children,* by Karen Gershon, published by Harcourt, Brace Jovanovich; pages 12–13, from *A Study in American Pluralism Through Oral Histories,* by Helen Epstein; pages 14–15, from *Thunder Out of China,* by Theodore White and Annalee Jacoby. Copyright © 1946 by William Sloane Associates, Inc. Renewed 1974 by Theodore H. White and Annalee Jacoby (William Morrow & Company); pages 22–23, 24, from *Refugees,* published by UNHCR; pages 31–32, from "Brave Words and Stark Survival," by Mehr Kamal, published by UNICEF *News;* pages 37–38, Amesty International; pages 44–45, 68–72, from *Caring About Refugees,* published by Christian Aid; page 47, Rosalynn Carter; pages 48–50, from Louisville *Courier-Journal.* Copyright 1979. Reprinted with permission; pages 54, 60–62, Tom Hoskins and Julie Forsythe, of the American Friends Service Committee; pages 55–57, Save the Children Fund; pages 64–65, Dr. Maureen McMullen.

Frontis photograph by V. Leduc/UNHCR

Copyright © 1982 by Gilburt D. Loescher and Ann Dull Loescher

LIBRARY OF CONGRESS CATALOGING IN PUBLICATION DATA
Loescher, Gil.   The world's refugees.
Bibliography: p.   Includes index.
SUMMARY: Explores the fate of the millions of people in contemporary society who have been uprooted and displaced by war, famine, drought, failing economy, political instability or oppression.   1. Refugees—Juvenile literature. [1. Refugees] I. Loescher, Ann Dull. II. Title.
HV640.L63   1982   362.8′2   82–47936
ISBN 0–15–299650–8

Printed in the United States of America   First edition   BCDE

To the caring and tireless workers
of The Save the Children Fund

UNHCR Worl

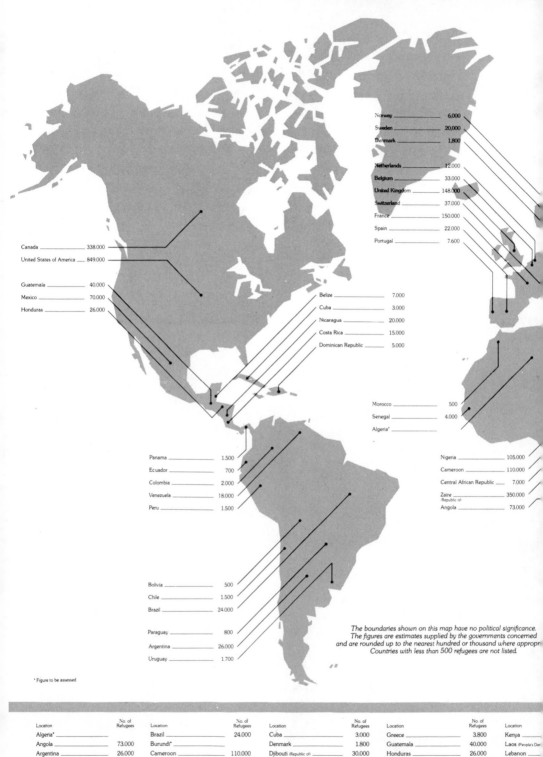

Norway — 6,000
Sweden — 20,000
Denmark — 1,800
Netherlands — 12,000
Belgium — 33,000
United Kingdom — 148,000
Switzerland — 37,000
France — 150,000
Spain — 22,000
Portugal — 7,600

Canada — 338,000
United States of America — 849,000

Guatemala — 40,000
Mexico — 70,000
Honduras — 26,000

Belize — 7,000
Cuba — 3,000
Nicaragua — 20,000
Costa Rica — 15,000
Dominican Republic — 5,000

Morocco — 500
Senegal — 4,000
Algeria*

Panama — 1,500
Ecuador — 700
Colombia — 2,000
Venezuela — 18,000
Peru — 1,500

Nigeria — 105,000
Cameroon — 110,000
Central African Republic — 7,000
Zaire Republic of — 350,000
Angola — 73,000

Bolivia — 500
Chile — 1,500
Brazil — 24,000

Paraguay — 800
Argentina — 26,000
Uruguay — 1,700

The boundaries shown on this map have no political significance.
The figures are estimates supplied by the governments concerned
and are rounded up to the nearest hundred or thousand where appropri
Countries with less than 500 refugees are not listed.

* Figure to be assessed

Location	No. of Refugees	Location	No. of Refugees	Location	No. of Refugees	Location	No. of Refugees	Location
Algeria*		Brazil	24,000	Cuba	3,000	Greece	3,800	Kenya
Angola	73,000	Burundi*		Denmark (Republic of)	1,800	Guatemala	40,000	Laos (People's Dem
Argentina	26,000	Cameroon	110,000	Djibouti (Republic of)	30,000	Honduras	26,000	Lebanon
Australia	304,000	Canada	338,000	Dominican Republic	5,000	Hong Kong	16,000	Lesotho
Austria	27,700	Central African Republic	7,000	Ecuador	700	India	3,300	Macau
Belgium	33,000	Chile	1,500	Egypt (Arab Republic of)	5,500	Indonesia	4,700	Malaysia
Belize	7,000	China	265,000	Ethiopia	11,000	Refugee Processing Centre	5,200	Mexico
Bolivia	500	Colombia	2,000	France	150,000	Italy	14,000	Morocco
Botswana	1,500	Costa Rica	15,000	Germany (Federal Republic of)	94,000	Japan	1,300	Netherlands

efugee Map

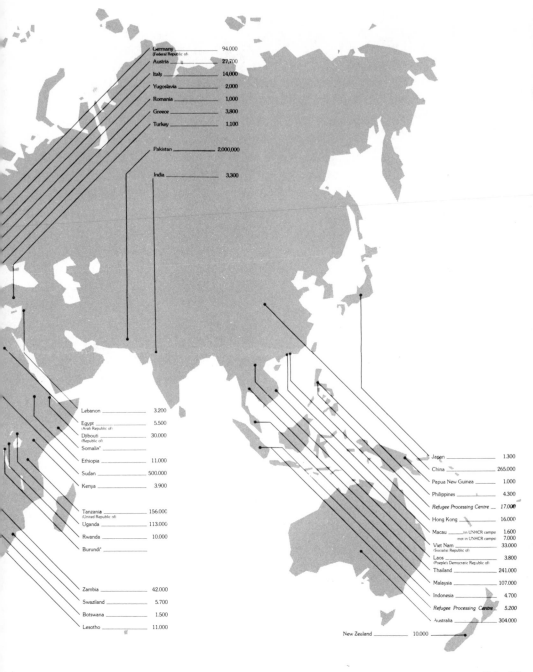

Germany (Federal Republic of) — 94.000
Austria — 27.700
Italy — 14.000
Yugoslavia — 2.000
Romania — 1.000
Greece — 3.800
Turkey — 1.100

Pakistan — 2.000.000

India — 3.300

Lebanon — 3.200
Egypt (Arab Republic of) — 5.500
Djibouti (Republic of) — 30.000
Somalia* —
Ethiopia — 11.000
Sudan — 500.000
Kenya — 3.900

Tanzania (United Republic of) — 156.000
Uganda — 113.000
Rwanda — 10.000
Burundi* —

Zambia — 42.000
Swaziland — 5.700
Botswana — 1.500
Lesotho — 11.000

Japan — 1.300
China — 265.000
Papua New Guinea — 1.000
Philippines — 4.300
Refugee Processing Centre — 17.000
Hong Kong — 16.000
Macau (in UNHCR camps) — 1.600 / (not in UNHCR camps) — 7.000
Viet Nam (Socialist Republic of) — 33.000
Laos (Poeple's Democratic Republic of) — 3.800
Thailand — 241.000
Malaysia — 107.000
Indonesia — 4.700
Refugee Processing Centre — 5.200
Australia — 304.000

New Zealand — 10.000

30 June 1981

Location	No. of Refugees	Location	No. of Refugees	Location	No. of Refugees	Location	No. of Refugees
New Zealand	10.000	Philippes	4.300	Swaziland	5.700	Uruguay	1.700
Nicaragua	20.000	Refugee Processing Centre	17.000	Sweden	20.000	Venezuela	18.000
Nigeria	105.000	Portugal	7.600	Switzerland	37.000	Viet Nam (Socialist Republic of)	33.000
Norway	6.000	Romania	1.000	Tanzania (United Rep of)	156.000	Yugoslavia	2.000
Pakistan	2.000.000	Rwanda	10.000	Thailand	241.000	Zaire (Republic of)	350.000
Panama	1.500	Senegal	4.000	Turkey	1.100	Zambia	42.000
Papua New Guinea	1.000	Somalia*		Uganda	113.000	Other countries in Africa	30.000
Paraguay	800	Spain	22.000	United Kingdom	148.000	Other countries in West. Asia	150.000
Peru	1.500	Sudan	500.000	United States of America	849.000	Other countries in East. Asia	3.000

CONTENTS

THE WORLD'S REFUGEES
A Test of Humanity

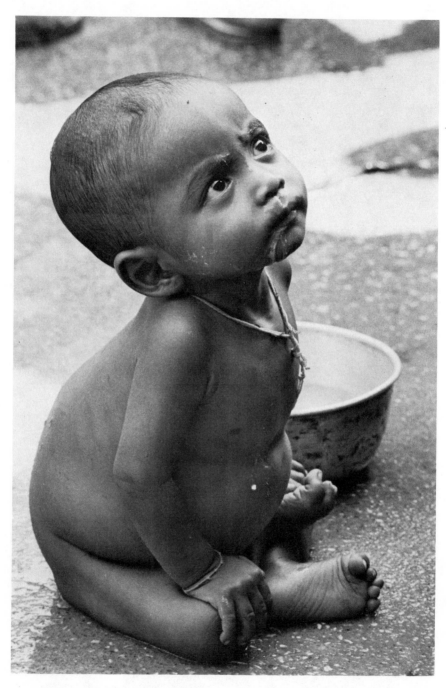

DOESN'T ANYBODY CARE?
(BRENDAN BEIRNE / THE SAVE THE CHILDREN FUND / U.K.)

1 · THE CENTURY OF Refugees

Refugees are among the world's most disadvantaged people. They have decided, or have been forced to decide, to leave the country in which they were born or now live. They are not immigrants. They do not voluntarily leave their homes to seek economic opportunity in another country. They are men, women, and children who have had to make one of the most difficult of all decisions: to cut their roots and flee from their homelands. They flee because of persecution or fear of it.

Many Vietnamese made that decision in the latter part of the 1970s. After thirty years of continuous conflict with the French and then with the Americans, Vietnamese Communists took control of all of Vietnam in 1975. Strict economic controls imposed by the Communist authorities created severe hardships for very many people. Thousands were sent from overcrowded cities to the jungle to cultivate new land and live in so-called "new economic zones." At the same time, over 200,000 members of the old government of South Vietnam were sent to prisonlike camps, called "re-education camps," to learn new political attitudes. These violations of basic human rights and the collapse in living standards created unbearable conditions and led to a massive exodus, both by land to China and by sea to the countries of Southeast Asia.

In the summer of 1979, the world's press and television screens were filled with heartrending photographs of the Vietnamese "boat people" who fled their Communist homelands in flimsy boats. A large percentage of them died before finding temporary shelter in refugee camps.

Vo Thi Tam was one of the lucky people who eventually made it to the United States. A few days after her arrival here, she told her story in the living room of a small house near Seattle, where she was staying with her sister's family. Tears streamed down her cheeks as she spoke:

My husband was a former officer in the South Vietnamese air force. After the fall of that government in 1975, he and all the other officers were sent to a concentration camp for re-education. When they let him out of the camp, they forced all of us to go to one of the "new economic zones," which are really jungle. There was no organization, there was no housing, no utilities, no doctor, nothing. They gave us tools and a little food, and that was it. We just had to dig up the land and cultivate it. And the land was very bad.

It was impossible for us to live there, so we got together with some other families and bought a big fishing boat, about thirty-five feet long.

Altogether, there were thirty-seven of us who were to leave—seven men, eight women, and the rest children. I was five months pregnant.

After we bought the boat we had to hide it, and this is how: We just anchored it in a harbor in the Mekong Delta. It's very crowded there, and very many people make their living aboard the boats by going fishing, you know. So we had to make ourselves like them. We took turns living and sleeping on the boat. We would maneuver the boat around the harbor, as if we were fishing or selling stuff, you know, so the Communist authorities could not suspect anything.

Besides the big boat, we had to buy a smaller boat in order to carry supplies to it. We had to buy gasoline and other stuff on the

OPPOSITE: OF THE THOUSANDS OF REFUGEES WHO FLED VIETNAM IN 1979, MOST SAILED ON FLIMSY BOATS IN THE HOPE OF REACHING SAFETY. THESE REFUGEES FROM VIETNAM ARE ON THEIR BOATS IN THE PORT OF BEIHAI, IN THE PEOPLE'S REPUBLIC OF CHINA. (A. CASELLA / UNHCR)

black market—everywhere there is a black market—and carry these supplies, little by little, on the little boat to the big boat. To do this we sold jewelry and radios and other things that we had left from the old days.

On the day we left we took the big boat out very early in the morning—all the women and children were in that boat, and some of the men. My husband and the one other man remained in the small boat, and they were to rendezvous with us outside the harbor. Because if the harbor officials saw too many people aboard, they might think there was something suspicious. I think they were suspicious anyway. As we went out, they stopped us and made us pay them ten taels of gold—that's a Vietnamese unit, a little heavier than an ounce. That was nearly all we had.

Anyway, the big boat passed through the harbor and went ahead to the rendezvous point where we were to meet my husband and the other man in the small boat. But there was no one there. We waited for two hours, but we did not see any sign of them. After a while we could see a Vietnamese Navy boat approaching, and there was a discussion on board our boat, and the end of it was that the people on our boat decided to leave without my husband and the other man. [Long pause.]

When we reached the high seas, we discovered, unfortunately, that the water container was leaking and only a little bit of the water was left. So we had to ration the water from then on. We had brought some rice and other food that we could cook, but it was so rough that we could not cook anything at all. So all we had was raw rice and a few lemons and very little water. After seven days we ran out of water, so all we had to drink was the sea water, plus lemon juice.

Everyone was very sick, and, at one point, my mother and my little boy, four years old, were in agony, about to die. And the other people on the boat said that if they were agonizing like that, it would be better to throw them overboard so as to save them pain.

During this time we had seen several boats on the sea and had waved to them to help us, but they never stopped. But that morning while we were discussing throwing my mother and son overboard, we could see another ship coming and we were very happy, thinking maybe it was people coming to save us. When the two boats were close together, the people came on board from there—it happened to be a Thai boat—and they said all of us had to go on the bigger boat. They made us all go there and then they began to search us—cutting off our blouses, our bras, looking everywhere. One woman, she had some rings she hid in her bra, and they undressed her and took out everything. My mother had a statue of Our Lady, a very precious one, you know, that she had had all her life—she begged them just to leave the statue to her. But they didn't want to. They slapped her and grabbed the statue away.

Finally they pried up the planks of our boat, trying to see if there was any gold or jewelry hidden there. And when they had taken everything, they put us back on our boat and pushed us away.

They had taken all our maps and compasses, so we didn't even know which way to go. And because they had pried up the planks of our boat to look for jewelry, the water started getting in. We were very weak by then. But we had no pump, so we had to use empty cans to bail the water out, over and over again.

That same day we were boarded again by two other boats, and these, too, were pirates. They came aboard with hammers and knives and everything. But we could only beg them for mercy and try to explain by sign language that we'd been robbed before and we had nothing left. So those boats let us go and pointed the way to Malaysia for us.

That night at about 9:00 P.M. we arrived on the shore, and we were so happy finally to land somewhere that we knelt down on the beach and prayed, you know, to thank God.

While we were kneeling there, some people came out of the woods and began to throw rocks at us. They took a doctor who was with us and they beat him up and broke his glasses, so that from that time on he couldn't see anything at all. And they tied him up, his hands behind him like this [demonstrates], and they beat up the rest of the men, too. They searched us for anything precious that they could find, but there was nothing left except our few clothes and our documents. They took these and scattered them all over the beach.

Then five of the Malaysian men grabbed the doctor's wife, a young woman with three little children, and they took her back into the woods and raped her—all five of them. Later, they sent her back, completely naked, to the beach.

After this, the Malaysians forced us back into the boat and tried

MOST SOUTHEAST ASIAN NATIONS HAVE BEEN RELUCTANT TO ACCEPT
VIETNAMESE REFUGEES. THESE VIETNAMESE HOPE THE PHILIPPINE GOV-
ERNMENT WILL NOT TOW THEM OUT.   (J. P. LAFFONT / UNHCR)

to push us out to sea. But the tide was out and the boat was so heavy
with all of us on board that it just sank in the sand. So they left us
for the night. . . .

In the morning, the Malaysian military police came to look over
the area, and they dispersed the crowd and protected us from them.
They let us pick up our clothes and our papers from the beach and
took us in a big truck to some kind of a warehouse in a small town
not far away. They gave us water, some bread, and some fish, and
then they carried us out to Bidong Island. . . .

Perhaps in the beginning it was all right there, maybe for ten
thousand people or so, but when we arrived there were already fifteen
to seventeen thousand crowded onto thirty acres. There was no housing, no facilities, nothing. It was already full near the beach, so we
had to go up the mountain and chop down trees to make room for
ourselves and make some sort of a temporary shelter. There was an

old well, but the water was very shallow. It was so scarce that all the refugees had to wait in a long line, day and night, to get our turn of the water. We would have a little can, like a small Coke can at the end of a long string, and fill that up. To fill about a gallon, it would take an hour, so we each had to just wait, taking our turn to get our Coke can of water. Sometimes one, two, or three in the morning we would get our water. I was pregnant, and my boys were only four and six, and my old mother with me was not well, but we all had to wait in line to get our water. That was just for cooking and drinking, of course. We had to do our washing in the sea.

The Malaysian authorities did what they could, but they left most of the administration of the camp to the refugees themselves, and most of us were sick. There were, of course, no sanitary installations, and many people had diarrhea. It was very hard to stop sickness under those conditions. My little boys were sick and my mother could hardly walk. And since there was no man in our family, we had no one to chop the wood for our cooking, and it was very hard for us just to survive. When the monsoons came, the floor of our shelter was all mud. We had one blanket and a board to lie on, and that was all. The water would come down the mountain through our shelter, so we all got wet.

After four months in the camp it was time for my baby to be born. Fortunately, we had many doctors among us, because many of them had tried to escape from Vietnam, so we had medical care but no equipment. There was no bed there, no hospital, no nothing, just a wooden plank to lie down on and let the baby be born, that was all. Each mother had to supply a portion of boiling water for the doctor to use and bring it with her to the medical hut when it was time. It was a very difficult delivery. The baby came legs first. But, fortunately, there were no complications. After the delivery I had to get up and go back to my shelter to make room for the next woman.

When we left Vietnam we were hoping to come to the United States, because my sister and her husband were here already. They came in 1975, when the United States evacuated so many people. We had to wait in the camp a month and a half to be interviewed, and then very much longer for the papers to be processed. Altogether we were in the camp seven months.

All this time I didn't know what had happened to my husband, although I hoped that he had been able to escape some other way and was, perhaps, in another camp, and that when I came to the United States I would find him.

We flew out here by way of Tokyo and arrived the first week in July. It was like waking up after a bad nightmare. Like coming out of hell into paradise. If only—[Breaks down, rushes from room.]

Shortly after she arrived in this country, Vo Thi Tam learned that her husband had been captured on the day of their escape and was back in a "re-education" camp in Vietnam.

We are shocked that a young woman like Vo Thi Tam should be an innocent victim of senseless persecution, forgetting that the plight of refugees is a universal, long-term problem that is as old as human history. From Biblical times till today they have been among the world's most enduring tragedies. Both the Old and New Testaments describe refugee movements. The Israelites fled from Pharoah's tyranny in Egypt to Canaan in the thirteenth century B.C. The Romans razed the city of Jerusalem in A.D. 70, forcing the Jews to flee. Until the twentieth century, most refugee movements were related to religious persecution, usually conducted against a particular group by the state. The word *refugee* was first used to describe the Protestant Huguenots, who fled religious repression in Roman Catholic France three hundred years ago and took refuge in scattered places all over the world.

■ *"Century of Refugees"*

In this century, people who fear persecution or death continue to leave their countries. Since the beginning of World War I, about 100 million people have been uprooted worldwide. They come from all sectors of society, and include small farmers, laborers, businessmen, professors, writers, artists, and members of religious and ethnic communities. The majority have been moved by force in large groups. Whole ethnic and religious groups have been traded by governments, expelled from their homelands, or forced to leave in the face of violence. Women and children often formed the largest part of these movements. The twentieth century is, as the German novelist Heinrich Böll once remarked, "the century of refugees and prisoners."

Millions of people were uprooted during the turbulent period between 1900 and 1925. During the Russian revolution of 1917 and the civil war of 1918–1920, more than 1.5 million people fled the country. Most of these refugees settled in Europe, China, and North America. During the same period, 500,000 Armenians left Turkey after 2 million of their countrymen were massacred in 1916. After the 1921–22 Greco-Turkish war, 1.25 million Greeks fled Asia Minor and sought refuge in Greece and southern Europe. After World War I, countless refugees wandered the globe and crowded such major European cities as Berlin, Vienna, Prague, and Paris. They jarred the consciences of individuals, governments, and voluntary organizations, all of which began emergency relief operations. The League of Nations helped develop cooperative international assistance for refugees and appointed a High Commissioner for Refugees in 1921. That was the first acknowledgment that refugees were entitled to international recognition and assistance. Over the next decade, several million displaced persons were given relief and resettled in forty countries. By the beginning of the 1930s, it was hoped that all major refugee problems would soon be solved through repatriation (returning to their own country) or resettlement in a new country.

■ Concentration Camps and Child Refugees

However, stability did not return and peace did not last. In 1933, Adolf Hitler came to power in Germany and began to put his terrible plans into effect. Hitler's intention was to establish a worldwide empire with himself as dictator. He started by taking over most of Europe. He also initiated a program to annihilate Jews. By 1938, news of Nazi concentration camps and extermination centers had begun to spread throughout Europe.

Peggy Mann, writing in the *Washington Post,* describes how men, women, even small children were cornered on the streets, beaten, whipped, and kicked by black-booted police. Rabbis were ordered to clean police toilets. Jewish women were forced down on their knees to scrub gutters, often with acid added to the scrub water. German civilians cooperated with the police by beating up Jews, evicting them, and looting their shops and homes. Such horrors produced a stream of German Jews who began to trickle and then pour out of Germany. This exodus reached major proportions after 1938, when the Nazis started what was to be known as "the final solution," a systematic attempt to eliminate all Jews from Germany and German-held lands.

In an effort to save their children from the Nazis, thousands of Jewish parents sent them out of Germany. Many children traveled by train and boat to the relative safety of Great Britain, where sponsors and temporary homes were found for these refugees. For most it was the beginning of a whole new life, because they never saw their parents or families again. Some of these people are still looking for relatives from whom they were separated forty-five years ago.

Several of these child refugees described their forced separation from parents and loved ones. Here a ten-year-old speaks of his last hours with his parents:

My mother took me to Berlin. When I left home my father was lying in bed ill; the concentration camp had damaged his health. He held me close and bade me look after my mother when she got to England in case he did not make it. I was then just ten years old. We got to Berlin to learn that I was too late for the first transport but would be able to go on the second. There was of course no money for me to go back home, so my mother took me to friends in Berlin, who kindly put me up [until the next transport]. My mother had to leave me there, and the last I ever saw of her was in Berlin Street, outside the friends' house, walking backward along the pavement to get a last look at me until she rounded the corner and we were parted.

A teenager describes what it was like to leave his parents forever:

I left home late in the evening with the whole family to see me off. At the station we were ushered into an enormous waiting room which was packed with children and parents weeping, crying, and shouting. It occurred to me there for the first time that our grief was no longer a personal one. We all belonged to a group, but not a group that was determined through social, economic or intellectual dividing lines: we were all refugees. We were ordered to take leave of our relatives quickly and go straight to the train; it had sealed windows, and once we were all inside it the doors were sealed as well. Shortly before the train was due to leave our relatives appeared again on the platform. From behind the sealed windows I saw my parents again, rigid and unsmiling like two statues, for the last time ever. I was sixteen years old.

In the confusion of the flight to safety, even brothers and sisters were separated forever.

Children under seven years old were meant to go to Holland, Belgium, and France. But my brother, who was only two, was allowed to come to England with me. When we were going from the train to the boat he was far ahead of me leading the long line of children. He looked like a drummer, with his chamberpot strapped onto his back. I was ten years old and had promised my mother to look after him. But as soon as we had said good-bye to our parents we were separated, and we never lived together again at all.

Many of these refugee children lived through exhausting and humiliating experiences:

At the frontier town of Aachen all Jews had to leave the train; all except myself were allowed to continue the journey. The reason for my being kept behind I can only guess at. I looked very "Aryan" at the age of fourteen, when my hair was still very light blonde. I was searched bodily by what seemed to me at the time an enormous woman, and my few belongings were turned upside down. I can only imagine that they thought that my family were taking advantage of the fact that I looked so un-Jewish and was still a child, and were trying to smuggle valuables out of the country. Whatever the reason, they were certainly looking for something, and it was a harrowing and terrifying experience for a child. The lining of my new warm gloves were ripped open; so was a new manicure set I had just had as a farewell present from a friend. My chocolates were squashed, and so on. Eventually, I was allowed to leave, after the officers or guards or whatever they were had even perused my diary, where I had vividly recorded my uncle's recent suicide, when the Gestapo came for him. I had secreted this in my case; naturally my parents would never have allowed me to take this, had they known. I now had to wait several hours for another train, then had to change trains in Brussels. I must have looked a bit forlorn, and a Belgian porter came and talked to me in Yiddish, which I could just barely understand. He was very nice and helped me get on the right train. The first "human being" since leaving my parents. . . . I arrived in London [England] at Victoria Station twelve hours late. My sister, who was meeting me there, was—not unnaturally—in a great state of agitation by then. I was so tired and dazed that I simply got out of the train and sat on my case on the platform, not even looking for her. My sister passed by me several times before realizing it was me. She was now living in London and had a little room in Euston. After cabling my arrival to my parents (I can guess what their state of mind must have been by then) we went by underground to her lodging, and I remember being greatly alarmed by the black uniforms of the underground guards, which reminded me of SS uniforms.

More lives were disrupted and people uprooted as the Nazis moved into Austria, Czechoslovakia, Poland, the Netherlands, and France. One Polish survivor recounts what it was like for him as a young boy when Germany invaded his country:

On September 6, 1939, I was awakened by my father. He said I had better get dressed; I had to leave to go to Warsaw. I got up and my mother was crying. She said the family should stay together, no matter what. And my grandfather was banging the table with a cane and yelling at my mother that she had no right for her own selfish reasons to have her son killed. And my mother yielded, packed a few rolls and salami, and stuffed a few zlotys in my pocket, and I was off [alone] on a dark street of Lodz going where everybody else was going. Until that time I never walked out of Lodz. There was just one big mass of humanity that was going out of Lodz on a highway which led to Warsaw.

We were continuously bombed on that road, because the civilians were intermingled with soldiers of the Polish army. Or maybe because the Germans felt like bombing civilians at that time; I don't know. Every time we heard aircraft approaching we would scatter to the sides of the highway and hide in the bushes and fields. After the bombers did their job, we would continue. That day I was absolutely sure that I would not get out alive. People were dying around me like flies. I survived by a sheer miracle. . . .

The number of refugees increased with the rise of Fascist dictatorships in Italy and Spain during the 1930s. Benito Mussolini and his brown-shirted army of hoodlums gained power in Italy by 1935, and life became so dangerous for the people who opposed him that nearly a million people fled from Italy. When Mussolini decided to invade the nearby country of Ethiopia that same year as part of his plan to conquer all Europe and North Africa, several thousand more homeless from Ethiopia were added to the world's refugee rolls.

In 1936 Spain was governed by an alliance of Liberal and Socialist Parties. The army leaders and right-wing parties feared that Spain might go further left, and therefore undertook an armed rebellion under General Franco to set up a Fascist dictatorship. Civil war broke out in Spain. Franco was helped by Hitler and Mussolini, and the Republican government of Spain, by Russia and thousands of volunteers from all over the world who formed the "International Brigade" to fight the Fascist forces. Franco won the long and bloody war. Leading Spanish Republicans were executed or imprisoned, though some fled abroad. By the time the conflict ended in 1939, some half million Spanish refugees had crossed the border to France. Many thousands of other Spaniards had died of starvation, disease, and "terror bombings" Franco and his German and Italian allies carried out against defenseless civilian populations.

But the horror had hardly begun. World War II pulverized European society and uprooted a large percentage of the world's population. During the war years, some forty million persons fled their homes. One in every eight Europeans became a refugee. Everyone suffered immensely, but especially Europe's

Jews. All over Eastern Europe the process of destruction went on. Entire communities perished overnight; families disappeared. Before World War II, the Jews of Europe were the intellectual and cultural center of world Jewry. By the end of the war, nearly six million Jews had been annihilated, mostly in the gas chambers of Nazi concentration camps. The number of Jewish children who died as a result of the war and persecution is believed to be about two million.

■ *Japan's War Machine*

In Asia during World War II, Japan played a role similar to that of Germany and Italy in Europe. Japan's economic resources were insufficient to maintain a rapidly growing population. She felt that she was treated as an upstart, and that the other Great Powers, particularly the United States and Great Britain, jealously resisted the fulfillment of Japan's aspirations. In response, Japan began to try to establish an economic and political sphere of influence and control in Asia, which would provide needed raw materials for a growing population and industrial undertakings. In 1931 Japanese leaders decided to invade the mainland of Asia. The terror bombing of Chinese cities and the deliberate pillage by invading Japanese troops caused millions of Chinese to leave their homes in search of safety. The American journalist Theodore White described the plight of refugees in Honan Province:

Peasants, sprawled about the station for acres, were waiting for the next train to take them away to the West and food. Most of them had come on trains that sneaked by the Japanese guns in the dark. Flatcars, boxcars, old coaches, were stuffed with people; tight huddles braced themselves on the roofs. It was freezing cold, and as the trains hurtled through the danger zone, the fingers of those who were clinging to the car roofs became numb; the weak fell under the steel wheels of the trains, and as we retraced their route later in the day, we saw their torn and bleeding bodies lying by the roadbed.

But most of the peasants were coming under their own power, by foot, by cart, by wheelbarrow . . . old women hobbled along on bound feet, stumbled and fell; no one picked them up. Other old women rode pickaback on the strong shoulders of their sons, staring through coal-black eyes at the hostile sky. Young men, walking alone, strode at a quicker pace, with all their possessions in a kerchief over their shoulder[s]. Small mounds of rags by the roadside marked where the weak had collapsed; sometimes a few members of a family stood staring at a body in silent perplexity. The children leaned on their staffs like old men; some carried bundles as large as themselves; others were dreamwalkers whose unseeing eyes were a thousand years old with suffering. Behind them all, from the land of famine a cold wind blew, sending the dust chasing them over the yellow plain. The march had been going on for weeks; it was to continue for weeks more.

■ Displaced Persons

After World War II, the massive dislocation of people in Europe and Asia generated renewed international concern. The United Nations Relief and Rehabilitation Agency (UNRRA) provided much-needed food, clothing, and medical supplies to refugees. It also became active in repatriation work. To a considerable extent, it succeeded in resettling the surviving victims of Nazi and Fascist persecution in new countries. Most of these people went to Israel, the United States, the Commonwealth countries, and West Germany. Only five months after the surrender of Germany in May 1945, UNRRA had repatriated seven million displaced persons with the help of volunteer organizations. However, refugees were often dissatisfied with the country they were sent to. Entire refugee populations were exchanged, sometimes against the will of the peoples involved. For example, thousands of Russians were forced to return to the Soviet Union, where many were sent to Siberian prison camps.

Moreover, some refugees were not permitted into the country they chose; many Jewish children underwent the journey to Palestine only to be turned back by the British.

In the thirty-five years since World War II, refugees have become a permanent feature of the world's landscape. International society has been marked by revolution, persecution, and war, and this trend shows no sign of moderating. Refugees seem to be an inevitable byproduct of such upheavals. No one pretends any longer that in one strong relief effort the refugee crisis can be made to disappear or even to be reduced to a few scattered individuals.

■ Communist Control in Eastern Europe

In the aftermath of World War II, Soviet-controlled governments took over in Eastern European countries. As a result, millions of Eastern Europeans fled to the West. The largest groups of these refugees left their homes in the late 1940s. At that time, Communist governments had gained control, but the physical barriers to escape had not yet been put up along the East-West borders. Thousands fled the campaigns of terror against suspected opponents of the new Communist regimes. Millions suffered forced relocation, imprisonment, exile, or execution.

The number of refugees from East to West was reduced with the effective sealing of Eastern European borders in the 1950s and the construction of the Berlin Wall in 1961. Nonetheless, other mass movements of people from Eastern Europe also occurred in the aftermath of the 1956 Hungarian uprising and the 1968 Czechoslovak crisis, both of which were crushed by Soviet troops. The combination of hope aroused by temporarily open borders and fear of reprisal motivated some 200,000 Hungarians and approximately 50,000 Czechs to leave their homes. In 1981 the Polish government responded to the Solidarity labor union movement by declaring martial law. Thousands of Poles had anticipated this crackdown and had migrated to the West.

■ Political Strife

Political upheavals on other continents created similar mass movements. After the partition of India in 1947 millions of Muslim and Hindu refugees fled religious strife. In the Middle East the creation of the state of Israel in 1948 absorbed most of Europe's remaining Jewish refugees, but from 700,000 to 900,000 Arabs whose ancestors had lived for generations in Palestine lost their lands and homes during the first Arab–Israeli war.

AFTER THE 1967 ARAB-ISRAELI WAR, PALESTINIAN REFUGEES WERE CON-
STANTLY MOVED FROM ONE CAMPSITE TO ANOTHER. THIS MAN'S DISTRESS
WAS TYPICAL OF THAT SUFFERED BY TENS OF THOUSANDS OF REFU-
GEES.   (SOUF / UNRWA)

There has been a longstanding debate about the cause of the
Palestinian refugee problem, with many Arabs saying the flight
was caused by Jewish terrorism, and many Jews saying it was
Arab policy. Whatever the cause, the Palestinian refugee sit-
uation remains at the center of the conflict between Arabs and
Jews that continues today.

In East Asia, Korea became the focus of international attention because of war and large numbers of refugees. At the end
of World War II, the United States President, Franklin D.

Roosevelt, and the Soviet leader, Joseph Stalin, agreed to temporarily divide former Japanese-occupied Korea into two parts. Russian forces occupied the northern part of Korea and American forces the southern part. As tensions between the United States and Russia increased after World War II, the temporary division of Korea became permanent. In North Korea, a repressive totalitarian state emerged under the leadership of Kim Il Sung. In South Korea, the authoritarian Syngman Rhee tried to form a government with the help of American advisers.

In 1950, North Korea invaded South Korea, and the United States Army entered the Korean War as part of the United Nations forces. During the course of the war, more than 5 million Koreans who refused to live under Communist control escaped by foot to South Korea.

■ World-Wide Upheavals

In the 1960s and 1970s, sudden and large movements of refugees occurred on almost all continents. In contrast to the situation in 1945, when refugees were located mainly in Europe, political upheavals throughout the world triggered major refugee migrations in Africa, Asia, and Latin America. These movements were larger and more complex than the earlier refugee movements.

Everywhere in the Third World nationalism triumphed. Colonial empires had drawn national boundaries that divided ethnic communities and created large minority groups in several African and Asian countries. The withdrawal from the Third World of such colonial powers as Britain, France, and the Netherlands ended at least some protection for these minorities. The newly independent governments, in an effort to create a consciousness of national identity, emphasized loyalty to the state. This dramatized the presence of minorities, who often became targets of persecution. Some governments exploited long-standing racial and religious prejudice and forced minority groups to flee. Some of the victims were Indians in East Africa, Chinese in Southeast Asia, Ibos in northern Nigeria, Hausas in Ghana,

BURMESE REFUGEES FLED RELIGIOUS AND POLITICAL PERSECUTION TO
NEARBY BANGLADESH.   (G. GORDON LENNOX / UNHCR)

and Togolese and Dahomeyans in the Ivory Coast, the Muslim
minority in Burma, and descendants of colonials in Africa and
Asia.

The continued political repression, economic underdevelopment, and civil and international conflict in the Third World
ensures that the problem of refugees will continue for the fore-
seeable future. Every year there are more refugees, with Africa,
Indochina, the Middle East, and the Caribbean the crisis points
contributing ever-increasing numbers of homeless people.

2 · THE WORLD *Refugee* CRISIS

We know from recent history that massive refugee movements can unbalance peace and stability in the world as much as any arms race or confrontation—whether it be political or military. For both humanitarian and political reasons we need to know more about the current world refugee problem.

In Chapter 1 we gave an historical account of refugee movements in the twentieth century. In Chapters 2 and 3 we will give an overview of the current number, location, and origin of the world's refugees. We will also describe the causes of refugee movements, the reasons why people are persecuted or suffer pain, and the reasons why people flee their homes to safety somewhere else.

In Chapter 4 we will describe the life and conditions in refugee camps and the hardships refugees suffer during prolonged stays there. Chapter 5 will deal with what is being done to help refugees and the difficulties these people experience in getting accustomed to new societies and new ways of life. Finally, in Chapters 6 and 7 we will describe past and present United States and international policies toward refugees, and we will suggest ways in which we in the United States and others in the international community can better respond to the global refugee crisis.

In recent years, much publicity has been given to the large numbers of refugees coming out of Indochina, Cuba, Poland, and the Soviet Union. But these people are only a small part of a much larger problem. There are about fifteen million refugees in the world today. Most of these are fleeing from one Third World country to another, placing enormous strains on economic, political, and physical resources already stretched near their limits.

■ Drought, Famine, Conflict

In Africa, refugees number in the millions. Instability, conflict, and tension mark domestic politics in many African countries. These, combined with drought and famine, have forced incredible numbers of people to migrate. Because of these conditions, Africa has the highest ratio of refugees to total population in the world.

In Northeast Africa drought, famine, the endless violence of the Ethiopian war, and Uganda's civil strife have endangered the lives of millions of people. In Somalia, Kenya, Djibouti, Eritrea, and the Sudan, hundreds of children and old people die every day.

Of the five million homeless Africans today, over one million are victims of the war in the Ogaden, in the Horn of Africa. These refugees are almost all nomadic tribal peoples escaping to Somalia from the Ethiopian war in the Ogaden. The Ogaden region, which borders Ethiopia and Somalia, is a vast grassland that has been a disputed territory ever since Somalia became independent in 1960. The region became a full-scale battlefield in 1977, when fighting broke out between Somali forces trying to annex the province and Ethiopian and Cuban troops opposing them. Ethiopia has dominated the struggle since 1978, but a bitter and long guerrilla war is still being fought, and people are still fleeing the region by the thousands.

The resulting refugee situation in Somalia is more than an emergency—it is a disaster. One out of every four inhabitants of this East African nation is a refugee. Thousands of new arrivals pour into refugee camps each week. Making matters worse is the fact that East Africa is one of the world's most drought-prone areas. In the summer of 1980, for example, it was officially estimated that about eight million people were in danger of losing their lives because of drought and war in the Horn of Africa and surrounding countries, including Uganda, Somalia, North Kenya, Djibouti, and Ethiopia.

Leon Davico, an official of the office of the United Nations High Commissioner for Refugees, had these impressions after a visit to refugee camps in the Horn of Africa in 1981:

In the Horn of Africa . . . there is drought. . . . I cannot shake from my mind images of a brief walk. . . . I see eyes of 20,000 people— men, women and children—gazing apathetically from skeletal figures; gazing without passion, without any apparent feeling of any kind.

They are hungry. They are thirsty. Most of them are ill.

THOUSANDS OF REFUGEES FLEE THE CONFLICT IN ERITREA. A MOTHER AND CHILD WAIT FOR FOOD TO BE DISTRIBUTED TO THEM IN A REFUGEE CAMP IN THE SUDAN. (SARAH ERRINGTON / UNHCR)

THE REFUGEE CRISIS IN SOMALIA HAS BEEN DESCRIBED AS THE "WORST OF ITS KIND IN THE WORLD." A MOTHER AND CHILD WAIT OUTSIDE AN INFANT FEEDING CENTER IN THE DARBI HORE CAMP. (THE SAVE THE CHILDREN FUND / U.K.)

Their food, when they can get it, is a kind of porridge made with cereal mixed with the polluted water of the only well in the region.

They are exiles from the tense situation in the Horn of Africa.

A supply plane is their lifeline. If it does not arrive on schedule, they start to count the dead.

"Yesterday we buried 15 people, mostly children"—I am told by a tall lean man. . . . His face and arms are covered with dust. He is so thin I can hardly believe it.

I see the children who have not yet died. Seated on the ground, close together, they seem to be trying to keep warm under the fierce heat of a hostile sun. They form long, horrific lines, waiting for a pitiful ration of this strange, unappetizing porridge. There is no shouting, none of the boisterous pushing and shoving we expect from children. They are not even crying. Too weak even to swat the flies that settle on their faces, they are silent.

The UNHCR publication *Refugees* tells the story of one lucky Somali famili who reached the safety of a refugee camp:

Fatima Mohamed Abdi is 23; she carries a baby in her arms—and is followed by her five other children, the oldest of whom is 9. She is a Marahan, a nomad of Somali ethnic origin; she arrived a few hours ago, crushed by the heat, a black turban her only protection against the sun. "We walked for two days to reach the frontier camp," she says, "with the other women of my family and the children; we just drank a little water—we couldn't find anything to eat."

The mounting catastrophe in Somalia is merely the most dramatic episode of a phenomenon that reaches every corner

IN NORTHWEST AFRICA, THREE QUARTERS OF THE POPULATION OF THE WESTERN SAHARA FLED TO DESERT CAMPS IN ALGERIA IN THE WAKE OF THE WAR THAT FOLLOWED THE PARTITION OF THEIR COUNTRY BY MOROCCO AND MAURITANIA. (FREDERICK SCHJANDER /UNHCR)

in Africa. For instance, in the northwest of Africa three quarters of the population of the Western Sahara fled to desert camps in Algeria in the wake of war, which followed the partition of their country by Morocco and Mauritania. Furthermore, on the west coast of the continent, nearly half the population of Equatorial Guinea went into exile in the 1970s in order to escape the brutality of their president, Francisco Macias Nguema. In southern Africa, escalating racial and political conflict, drought, and unemployment have resulted in the flight of an estimated one million people from their homes.

Every year tens of thousands of black men from neighboring African countries leave their families to work in South Africa. The mines, factories, and large farms in South Africa need cheap labor. Employers pay migrant workers shockingly low wages because blacks are desperately poor and jobs are scarce. The South African government does not permit migrants or its own black male citizens to bring their families with them when they work in the mines or the cities.

Eight years ago Mnsiki Zwani decided to leave his wife, Khatsele, and eight children in Swaziland to work in South Africa's gold mines. Mnsiki sends money home three times a year—between $130 and $250 each time. Mnsiki's last visit home was six months ago. His visits are so infrequent that now the smallest of the eight children does not recognize him when he comes home. Mrs. Zwani seems resigned to the estrangement from her husband. "Of course I wish he were here. He could do the ploughing and the harder work as he did before. But I'm used to it now. He will probably have to go on working in the mines until his strength is exhausted."

There is no solution in sight to Africa's refugee problem. The political and social turmoil that has characterized that continent since the early 1960s has not yet run its course. While the international media has focused on a few of the conflicts throughout the continent, the plight of Africa's millions of refugees has largely escaped world attention. A combination of poor communication and the inaccessibility of refugee camps has helped to obscure from outside scrutiny the seriousness of the refugee situation in Africa.

EVERY YEAR THOUSANDS FLEE THE CONFLICT IN WHITE-MINORITY-RULED NAMIBIA AND TAKE SHELTER IN CAMPS IN ANGOLA. THESE REFUGEES COME WITH VERY FEW BELONGINGS AND LIVE A MEAGER EXISTENCE. (G. GORDON-LENNOX / UNHCR)

■ *Succession of Hostilities*

During the past several years in Southeast and South Asia, people have swept across borders in search of refuge. The war, worsening economic conditions, violations of human rights, and conflicts between ethnic groups have caused several million people to leave their homes.

The refugee crisis in Indochina has, more than any other refugee crisis, captured the attention of the world. This may be because of America's long-standing involvement in Vietnam. Indochina's refugees are the victims of a succession of wars and revolutions. During the American war in Vietnam, several million people migrated from the Vietnamese, Cambodian, and Laotian countryside into the cities and refugee camps. Peasants were either driven into the cities by bombing and shelling or attracted to urban life by the hope of better living conditions. For example, between 1972 and 1975, the population of Saigon increased from 1.8 million to 3.8 million as a result of such migration. By the war's end in 1975, the majority of the rural population had moved into the cities. The economic effects of these massive transfers of refugees and migrants were devastating to the rural economy, and all three countries had severe resettlement problems.

After the United States withdrawal and the victories of the Indochinese Communists, the region continued to be shaken by one violent convulsion after another. In 1976 Vietnam was reunited, but there was no reconciliation between people from former North and South Vietnams. The Communist authorities excluded from the new society large sections of the southern population. By the most conservative estimate, 200,000 people were imprisoned without trial for indefinite periods in "re-education" camps. The families of these prisoners were denied civic rights. At the same time, severe economic problems—caused by poor Socialist planning and the cost of keeping one million men under arms and a quarter of them fighting in Laos and Cambodia—resulted in considerable hardship for the majority of Vietnamese people.

In an attempt to consolidate power after 1975, Laotian Communists, with the help of the Vietnamese army, imprisoned tens of thousands of Laos for indefinite periods. They also fought a ruthless war to drive highland people into the plains, where they could be collectivized and controlled.

In Cambodia, the Pol Pot regime seized power in 1975 and, with the backing of China, embarked on radical economic and social programs. The Pol Pot Khmer Rouge murdered about two million Cambodians in order to rid the country of unwanted people. They also systematically destroyed Buddhist temples and imprisoned and murdered Buddhist monks.

In late 1978 Vietnam invaded Cambodia to overthrow the Pol Pot regime and replace it with a Cambodian government that was more responsive to Vietnamese interests. This action angered China, and in early 1979 China attacked Vietnam in order to prevent Hanoi from consolidating power in Cambodia.

These two festering regional wars together with rapid political and economic changes in the region generated new streams of refugees.

Under such conditions, it is not surprising that between 1975 and 1980 more than 1.5 million Indochinese fled their native countries by sea and over land. Tens of thousands set out to sea in rickety boats. Most Americans have heard about the Vietnamese boat people, going from port to port, being towed in leaky fishing boats from harbors and beaches, back out to high seas. Also, most Americans were shocked by the specter of mass murder and mass starvation in Cambodia. As a result of war, famine, and the massive blood-letting of Pol Pot's Khmer Rouge, the total population of Cambodia was reduced by almost half in less than ten years. Beginning in the spring of 1979, huge numbers of Cambodians walked out of their country. They traveled by night, avoiding land mines and ambush—without food and weakened by malaria and dysentery. They walked for days or weeks, always in search of edible plants and tree bark to sustain themselves, until they reached the Thai border.

Perhaps less well known is the situation of the H'mong, hill tribesmen from Northern Laos who once fought for the CIA in Laos. When the change to a Communist government came in Laos, the H'mong chose to resist. Eventually, they ran out of ammunition, and the mountains where they lived were surrounded by Laotian and Vietnamese Communist forces. They were bombed, gassed, and relentlessly pursued by Communist troops. The H'mong began to flee to the Mekong River and the Thai border, which was about a month's walk away. They ate roots and leaves along the way. Those without teeth, young children and the elderly, died of starvation before they could cross the Mekong to Thailand.

Also in Southeast Asia, on a remote island off Indonesia, thousands of refugees have starved to death. Many Westerners have never heard of East Timor or its famine, but some veteran relief workers have compared it to Cambodia in its severity, if not in its size. The facts are incredible. Since 1975 over 100,000 Timorese out of an estimated population of 690,000 are believed

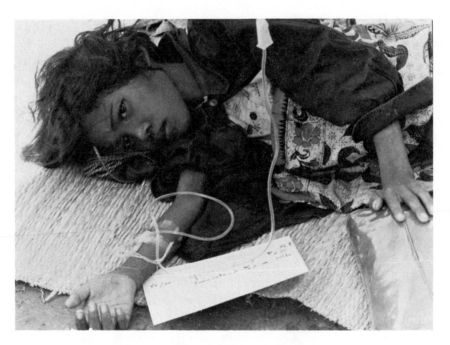

MOST OF THE REFUGEES WHO ARRIVED AT SA KAEO HAD TO UNDERGO MEDICAL TREATMENT. SOME WERE SO WEAK FROM STARVATION THEY COULD BE FED ONLY INTRAVENOUSLY. (K. GAUGLER / UNHCR)

to have died at the hands of the Indonesian military or as a result of starvation. Malnutrition afflicts many; and a large number of children may be facing permanent brain damage because of hunger.

The causes of this tragedy are both military and political. In 1975 Portugal withdrew from what had been until then its colony of East Timor. In the same year, Indonesia used military force to try to annex the country. What followed was a war between the left-wing independence guerrilla movement, called Fretilin, and a well-equipped Indonesian army.

In response to continuing resistance by Fretilin, the Indonesian military forced the Timorese population to leave their homes in the mountains and take refuge in camps, while Indonesia bombed the mountain areas. The bombing prevented the Timorese from growing their own food, with the result that there occurred widespread starvation. While the United Nations has consistently called for the withdrawal of Indonesian forces, major Western nations, including the United States, Britain, and Australia, have not criticized Indonesian actions for fear of damaging important trading links and security interests with Indonesia. Today the war has abated, but not ended. Progress towards alleviating the plight of the Timorese people has been slow. Timorese refugee problems—hunger, disease, and the loss of their human rights—cry out for immediate attention.

■ Soviet Invasion

For centuries the warrior tribesmen of Afghanistan have migrated down from the mountains of Central Asia to the plains of the Indian subcontinent. Today another migration is taking place across this wild frontier. In December 1979 the Afghanistan government of President Hafizullah Amin was overthrown in a military coup. The new President, Babrak Karmal, with the aid of Soviet troops, sought to consolidate power throughout the country. Fleeing the advance of the Soviet military, nearly two million Afghans sought refuge in makeshift camps inside neighboring Pakistan. Over the past three years, Soviet occupation forces have ruthlessly attacked villages, bombing houses, mowing down tribesmen from helicopter gunships, defoliating forest cover, and sowing the land with mines and lethal booby traps. Homeless and unable to cultivate their fields, thousands of refugees have flocked across the borders with Pakistan and Iran. Others have fled because of what is perceived to be a genuine threat to their freedom to practice their Islamic faith. Most of the refugees are women, children, and old men. They travel a dangerous route using mountainous footpaths. Still other angry tribesmen remain behind in Afghanistan to join the resistance forces, called the mujahideen, or "holy warriors." They hope to free their country from Soviet control and to restore its Islamic tradition.

One Afghan refugee is ten-year-old Shah Zarina. Along with her grandmother and four younger brothers and sisters, she left her ancestral village in Jalalabad Province after her father,

IN THE WAKE OF THE DECEMBER 1979 SOVIET INVASION OF AFGHANISTAN, 2 MILLION AFGHANS HAVE SOUGHT REFUGE IN MAKESHIFT CAMPS INSIDE NEIGHBORING PAKISTAN. MOST OF THE REFUGEES ARE WOMEN, CHILDREN, AND OLD MEN. THESE CHILDREN STAND IN FRONT OF THEIR SHELTER AT THE PISHIN REFUGEE CAMP.   (BOCCON-GIBOD / SIPA / UNHCR)

who had joined the fighting against the new Soviet-controlled government, was killed. Her older brother, Ahmed Shah, escorted them to a refugee camp in Pakistan and then returned to Afghanistan to fight. According to Mehr Kamal in *UNICEF News*:

The family was fairly well off in Afghanistan and managed to bring along some gold ornaments, a couple of wristwatches and a few goats. All through the first winter they huddled under two blankets issued to them by the Pakistan authorities in a tent which they shared with three other families. The family received four rupees (around 40 cents) for each person per day to buy essential food.

Now the ornaments are all gone—sold to buy food, clothes and other urgent necessities. So are the wristwatches, the blankets and all but two of the goats. One of the younger children died some months ago, the other three are constantly sick. The bitter winter cold causes bronchitis and fever, which has taken over from the attacks of malaria, dysentery and dehydration, which affected them during the intense heat of summer.

■ *Civil War*

Perhaps the greatest exodus of refugees in history took place in Bangladesh in 1971. Longstanding ethnic and political differences between the Bengalis of East Pakistan and the Punjabi rulers of West Pakistan led to civil war in 1971. The Punjabi authorities tried to restore order in East Pakistan by brute force. Terrified at the repression of the Punjabi-led forces, some ten million East Pakistanis fled into neighboring India. After India

MALNOURISHED BURMESE REFUGEE CHILDREN RECEIVE VITAMIN BISCUITS DISTRIBUTED BY THE LOCAL RED CROSS IN BANGLADESH. (G. GORDON-LENNOX / UNHCR)

intervened in the conflict and defeated West Pakistan, the Bengali refugees were successfully sent home, and East Pakistan was renamed Bangladesh.

■ *Violence in the Middle East*

Refugees are also a major feature of life in the Middle East. Current estimates put the total number of refugees in that area between 3.5 and 4 million. This enormous number results from the wars, revolutions, coup d'états, persecutions, and other forms of violence that have become a way of life in this part of the world.

The plight of Palestinians is one of the world's longest-lasting refugee problems, its history dating back several decades. It lingers along with efforts to achieve an acceptable Middle East peace settlement. In all, 1.8 million Palestinians lost their homes and livelihoods as a result of the establishment of Israel in 1948 and three subsequent Mideast wars. Dispossessed of their homeland, Palestinians have become entangled in Middle East politics, and the resolution of the Palestinian issue remains a seemingly intractable international problem.

Elsewhere in the Middle East there are numerous other refugee groups. In Lebanon, Christians have fought other Christians as well as Muslims, and over 500,000 persons were homeless as of 1982. Iraq's invasion of Iran in 1980 and Iran's counter-invasion of Iraq in 1982 drove over a million people away from their homes. The island of Cyprus has a Turkish ethnic minority and a Greek minority who have fought a long civil war. Since Cyprus gained its independence from Britain in 1960, Turks and Greeks have been unable to develop a satisfactory working relationship. As a result, violence has broken out intermittently. Following a round of bloody ethnic fighting in 1974, the island was partitioned. Then 160,000 Greeks were moved south, and 40,000 Turks north, of the demarcation line.

Still another tragedy in the Middle East are the many homeless Kurds. They are non-Arab Muslim people living in several Middle Eastern nations, in all of which they are a minority.

LOSING HER TENT DURING THE WINTER STORMS OF FEBRUARY 1969 WAS
A MAJOR TRAGEDY FOR THIS DISPLACED PALESTINIAN WHO FOUND SHELTER
IN BAQAA EMERGENCY CAMP IN JORDAN.   (MUNIR NASR /UNRWA)

The Kurdish people seek recognition of their rights to the
homelands they have occupied for centuries. Unfortunately,
they have often been victims of complicated international power
plays and have had to flee persecution in Iraq and Iran as well
as in other states.

■ Repression Closer to Home

The refugee situations in Central and South America have also contributed to the worldwide problem, but they have particular significance for the United States because most of these refugees try to flee to this country. In Latin America, political factors dominate as the major cause of displacement. In some instances there are economic factors, too. Political causes range from bloody civil wars to dissatisfaction with the politics, economics, or social systems of various regimes.

Political strife, with citizens and governments locked in life-or-death struggles between forces of political extremes, often results in repression, terrorism, and torture. Such strife has created instability and tense political climates throughout Central and South America. Countries controlled by military and right-wing regimes, such as El Salvador, Guatemala, Argentina, Uruguay, and Chile have instituted severely repressive policies against left-wing opponents and those suspected of disloyalty. In these countries, thousands of persons have been killed or have "disappeared" while they were in the hands of security forces. The "crimes" of these people were that in a desire to improve life in their villages or neighborhoods, they had associated with political opposition groups, peasant leagues, labor unions, or clergy. Things we take for granted can put one's life in danger in many countries in Central and South America. Farming and improving one's land, joining a labor union and bargaining for higher wages and improved working conditions, or active political participation may be considered crimes in some countries. The choices for many of these people are to stay at home and cease their opposition in hope of surviving, or to leave. If they leave, they lose their land, crops, close family ties, roots, and everything they have struggled to build. In spite of this, thousands have chosen to flee to neighboring countries because they feared for their lives.

In 1971, for example, the military took control in Chile. The president was murdered. The Congress was dissolved, and all political parties were disbanded. A curfew was imposed and the press was censored. The secret police were given unlimited

A REFUGEE CHILD IN ARGENTINA OUTSIDE HER SCHOOL. LATIN AMERICANS WHO HAVE BEEN FORCED TO FLEE TO NEIGHBORING COUNTRIES OFTEN FIND ONLY A PRECARIOUS TEMPORARY REFUGE AND MUST MOVE ON TO THIRD COUNTRIES. THE UNCERTAINTY AND, OFTEN, DANGER REFUGEES ARE EXPOSED TO UNDER THESE CONDITIONS HAS BEEN PARTICULARLY TRAUMATIC FOR THE CHILDREN. (JIM BECKET /UNHCR)

power, and thousands of people were tortured or killed. Books were burned and the universities were administered by the army. Thousands of Chileans fled to other countries. It is almost impossible to imagine the upheaval of these events. If what happened in Chile in the wake of the military coup in 1971 had occurred in the United States, 25 million Americans would have become refugees, 100,000 would have disappeared, and 2 million would have been killed. No one's life would have been unchanged.

In Central America, similar events have been occurring since the late 1970s. The 1978–79 civil war in Nicaragua toppled President Anastasio Somoza. The United Nations High Commissioner for Refugees reported that "out of a total population of . . . 2.5 million, 150,000 were killed or wounded, some 100,000 became refugees and half were forced to abandon their homes." In 1980 most of the refugees returned to Nicaragua from neighboring countries, but 100,000 Nicaraguans are believed to be in California, Florida, and elsewhere in the United States.

In neighboring El Salvador, the following accounts by peasants tell of the repression by right-wing government forces in that country. These were published in Spanish in *Solidaridád,* the international bulletin of the Legal Aid Office of the Archbishopric of San Salvador. They were translated into English by Amnesty International, the human rights organization that was awarded the Nobel Peace Prize in 1977:

I live in Jicaro, near Las Minas. . . . On Tuesday, 13th May [1980], as I was beginning to prepare a small plot of land for planting corn, I realized that an armed helicopter had been flying over the area since the early hours of the morning. A few minutes later, I saw about nine hundred National Guardsmen, soldiers and members of ORDEN [national security police] coming into Jicaro. . . . A peasant named Salomon Alag was sowing corn. When they saw him, they shot him; then they killed José Melgar and his wife Josefina Guardado, Salvadór Alas, Jesús Mena and two others. People began to flee towards the mountains in the direction of the valley of Los Brizuela. There the soldiers dragged Adrian Brizuela from his home and shot him in the street. They also took out his brother Hermenegildo, brutally beat him up and, thinking he was dead, left him lying in the street. There were about five hundred of us fleeing, including old people, women and children. . . . We arrived at the village of El Potrero at about two o'clock in the afternoon and from there we saw the guards pushing rocks down El Pajal hill in order to kill some women and children who were down below. Amongst our group, Amadeo Mejia and three children of eleven, seven and five years old were shot. We did not go on because [we] were afraid they were waiting for us so we decided to spend the night in Jocote Redondo mountain, putting up with the cold, hunger and the heavy storm which broke out that night. A three-month-old baby died from the cold. At dawn, we carried on . . . but a helicopter, the Army and National Guard were following us closely . . . we heard heavy shooting coming from the direction of the Sumpul river and saw several helicopters flying over the area, so we again went up into the mountains and spent the night there.

Another eyewitness describes what happened to his group of peasants while they were fleeing government troops at the Sumpul River, on the border of El Salvador and Honduras:

We had been there for about an hour when we were attacked from all sides. Two olive-green helicopters attacked us from the air and more than five hundred National Guardsmen (Salvadorean government troops) blocked all exits. The only way we could escape was by crossing the river Sampul in the direction of Honduras. During this attack, more than twenty-five people were machine-gunned. When I entered the swollen river, I saw seven children who had drowned being dragged downstream by the strong current. One of them was about six or seven months old. Some children stayed on the Salvadorean side and the mothers watched from the Honduran side as a National Guard from our country threw several little children into the river, threatening to throw more if we did not return to the Salvadorean side. A Honduran soldier shot at the National Guard and said what was happening was not the children's fault; that it was the fault of the National Guardsmen because they were provoking the peasants. About half an hour later, the Honduran authorities told us to swim back across the river to our country. When we returned, we were tied up by the thumbs and made to lie face down. We were kicked and beaten with rifles for eight hours. At about half past five in the afternoon, we were told that old people and some women and children would be set free.

Those of us who were set free, about seventeen of us, went up into the mountains leaving about twenty-five people still captured. We had been up in the mountains for about fifteen minutes when we heard heavy shooting near the river. Without doubt the Guardsmen and soldiers assassinated those we had left behind.

■ *Political Persecution and Failing Economies*

In neighboring Cuba, over a million of Cuba's ten million people have left that Caribbean island since Fidel Castro took power in 1959. Most have settled in the Miami, Florida, area. During the Castro government's early years, dissatisfaction with the Communist political and economic system was the predominant cause of the exodus of hundreds of thousands from Cuba. In recent years, however, difficult economic conditions and the desire to join relatives in the United States and elsewhere have become added incentives for many Cubans to go into exile.

Elsewhere in the Caribbean, hundreds of thousands of Haitians have departed from their homeland during the twenty-three years the Duvalier family has ruled that island. Haitians leave for a variety of political and economic reasons. Haiti is the most impoverished nation in the Western hemisphere. Its annual gross national product is less than $150 per capita. Government spending is skewed, with a very high proportion spent on national defense and a very small proportion on education and health.

President-for-life Jean Claude Duvalier ("Baby Doc") has maintained total control over the government of Haiti since 1971. Although he is reputed to be less harsh than his father, François Duvalier ("Papa Doc"), his regime is nonetheless severely repressive. The human rights record of Haiti is abysmal. Haitian refugees often speak of arbitrary arrests, beatings, confiscation of property, imprisonment of opposition political leaders, and execution of relatives by the dreaded secret police, called the Ton Ton Macoutes. To speak badly of the Haitian government is a punishable crime. Haitian prisons are notorious for unsanitary conditions and the widespread practice of torture. In the face of such a terrifying political situation and in hopes of improving their own standard of living, many Haitians, like the Vietnamese, have set out to sea in overcrowded boats to seek refuge in other countries, particularly the United States and the Bahamas. Many boats never make it. On the 800-mile voyage to Florida's east coast, some Haitians starve to death or die from lack of drinking water. In several cases, boats have overturned on the high seas and all passengers aboard have drowned.

The Haitians who leave their country today say they are fleeing a government that practices arbitrary imprisonment, torture, extortion, and takeovers of private land by government officials. One typical story is the case of Julie, who was a prosperous businesswoman in Haiti. She owned her own house and always had enough food to eat. Two members of the Ton Ton Macoute insisted on buying on credit and never paid their bills. Her son, who was in the military, reported them to the authorities. When the Macoutes found out that Julie had taken part in the complaint, they said they would kill her. She fled her home in Port-Au-Prince and got on a boat to Miami. Later, she learned that the Macoutes had jailed her son for informing on them.

Far more terrifying is this account by Merilien Menzious:

IN 1980 OVER 120,000 CUBANS FLED BY BOAT TO FLORIDA. AFTER A LONG SEPARATION, THIS CUBAN REFUGEE FAMILY WAS REUNITED BY THE INTERNATIONAL RESCUE COMMITTEE. (INTERNATIONAL RESCUE COMMITTEE)

I was arrested upon my return to Haiti in 1977, imprisoned in Casernes Dessalines and Fort Dimanche (prisons), repeatedly beaten until near death, and released only by paying a bribe. My passport, money, and belongings were confiscated by Haitian officials at Port-au-Prince airport, from which I was taken to Casernes Dessalines. I had returned from the Bahamas, where I had been working for many years because my aunt was in the hospital and needed my help to pay her medical bills. It was a Monday in mid-February.

At the prison I was told, "You were away because you are political against Duvalier. Your father was for Dèjoie (opposition candidate in 1957), and as a student you threatened Duvalier (I was ten years old at the time)." Then they beat me, and I was beaten again that night at Fort Dimanche, where I was transferred at about 6 P.M.

From Tuesday until Saturday, I was beaten twice daily, mornings and evenings, each day by a different guard. I regularly lost consciousness, and soon could barely move at all. Not once was I given food or water in six days. My cell measured about three feet in width by three and a half feet in length. It was impossible to lie down.

The guard who beat me would open the door and start hitting me on the body and head with a club and kicking me severely, knocking me back into the cement wall. I was bleeding all over my face and on the back of my head. I later lost six teeth due to these beatings.

Thursday morning, before separating to beat us, I heard one of the guards say to the others, "Some here are from Miami. One is from the Bahamas. They're political—against Duvalier. We have to kill them." Day and night I heard the crying of the other prisoners.

On Saturday morning, instead of beating me, the guard asked me if I had any money. "If you do, I'll help you, because they are ready to kill you." I gave him the $50.00 I had sewn into my shorts, which I still had on. He returned at midnight, took me to the airport, put me on a plane to the Bahamas, and, as I later learned, gave my passport to the pilot of the plane.

In the Bahamas, I was in and out of the hospital in Nassau for about four months. My ribs were damaged. My forehead and the back of my head were swollen and inflamed. They had to cut off my eyebrows. They operated on my forehead and on the back of my head to remove excess blood.

Despite personal stories like this one, the United States government regards nearly all Haitians as nonrefugees and tries to send Haitians who arrive in this country back to Port-Au-Prince.

■ *Communist Rule*

Meanwhile, across the world in the Eastern Hemisphere, the Soviet Union and the Communist countries of Eastern Europe are sources of more millions of refugees. People leave Communist-ruled countries for a number of reasons, including the lack of personal freedom and of economic opportunity. These refugees are often victims of persecution by authorities for their political views, religious beliefs, or family backgrounds. Many younger people feel that their chances for economic advancement are much better in the West than at home. Most of these refugees have sought resettlement in Western Europe and North America.

Authorities in Communist countries strictly regulate emigration and allow only selected people to leave. The procedure for emigrating is difficult and is complicated in many cases by inexplicable delays and red tape. Not only are many applications for exit permits turned down, but applying to leave the country exposes a citizen to possible reprisals, among them loss of one's job, denial of permission to reside in a certain place, and endless harassment, including systematic surveillance and even beatings. Nevertheless, thousands of Soviet and East European Jews have been allowed to leave for Israel and the West. Ethnic Germans in the Soviet Union, Poland, Rumania, and elsewhere have been permitted to go to West Germany, but many more would like to leave. The Universal Declaration of Human Rights and international agreements such as the Helsinki Accords were supposed to promote the free flow of people across national borders. Regardless of this, many people in the Eastern-bloc nations are not allowed freedom of emigration.

■ *A Global Problem*

As we begin a new decade filled with unrest and uncertainty, refugees remain a constant reminder to the world community of the unsatisfactory political situations that prevail in most countries today. Merely reciting the numbers of refugees worldwide barely sketches the enormity of the problem. Refugees need to be fed, clothed, and sheltered. They need to find new homes if they cannot return to their old ones. They want to go back home if they can, and often need help to do so.

3 · Refugees IN TRANSIT

Refugees are almost always forced to flee through little fault of their own. Often they have not planned or prepared for the journey, and usually their departure is hurried, with no time to pack or gather possessions and money. Caught between danger at home and loss of identity in a strange land, they seek safety in societies where they are isolated, different, and often impoverished. Solomon is one of these people.

Solomon is a black South African refugee. He has left his home and family in Soweto, near Johannesburg, to go to Botswana. He is only fourteen years old. In 1976 Solomon and his school friends organized and attended a peaceful demonstration protesting the school curriculum for black children in South Africa. When the South African police killed some of the students and arrested many others, Solomon was frightened. He was also angry because black people have little freedom in South Africa. He decided to leave home to settle in a country where he could get a good education. Then he might be able to work for change in South Africa.

Solomon could not pack a suitcase and fly out of the country on an airplane. He did not have enough money to do that, and he did not want to be caught by the police. So he just put some food and an extra sweater in a cloth bag and caught a train to a town near the border with Botswana. He could not use the road to walk out of the country because the police have a station at the border. Instead, he walked many miles into the bush and then had to wade across a river into Botswana.

Solomon now lives in a refugee camp in Botswana. Life is boring for people in the camp. There are no schools to attend and no games to play. Solomon has no family there. He hopes that this situation is temporary. He would like to move on to another country in Africa to continue with his education.

■ *Flight From Danger*

Few refugees give thought to the consequences of flight or to the frightening experiences awaiting them once they leave home. Perhaps the most dramatic example of people who have suffered immense personal hardship in their flight from danger are the Indochinese. As we have seen, Indochinese refugees cannot

SOUTH AFRICAN REFUGEES IN A CAMP IN BOTSWANA RECEIVE THEIR DAILY RATION OF GRUEL. (UNHCR)

simply cross a frontier to safety but risk their lives in the effort to escape. For example, it takes the H'mong nearly a month to walk from their mountain villages in Laos to the Mekong River. They travel in small family groups. Those who become too sick or too weak to continue must be left behind on the jungle path.

The following story describes dangers the H'mong encounter. One mother, traveling with her four children, was ambushed on the path leading to the Mekong River. Her fifteen-year-old daughter was critically wounded, and it was evident that she could not continue. Afraid of capture by the soldiers, the daughter begged her mother to kill her. The mother gave her daughter a poisonous plant to eat and sat under a tree with her until the child died. Then she and the other children continued down the path leading to the Mekong River.

In Cambodia, escaping refugees must spend weeks in the jungle avoiding mined trails and Communist patrols. Consequently, many are cut down in crossfire or die of exhaustion and starvation before ever reaching the border. Casualties are probably highest among the Vietnamese refugees who set out to cross the South China Sea in small boats never intended for such voyages. On most of those boats, only half of those who set sail ever reach land again.

■ Children as Refugees

Such harrowing experiences affect children most. Refugee children who have been uprooted from familiar surroundings and taken to a new locale under violent conditions have lived through a nightmare and are often permanently affected. This is particularly true of Cambodian children. From 1975 to 1979, huge numbers of Cambodians, perhaps millions, were killed arbitrarily. Only when we realize that probably there is not a single Cambodian refugee in the United States who knows that his entire family is left alive can we begin to understand the enormity of what has happened. The upheaval of recent events in Cambodia has been especially traumatic for the youngest of the victims. After visiting refugee camps in Thailand in 1979, Mrs. Rosalynn Carter commented:

. . . I witnessed incredible starvation, disease, dislocation and suffering. At the Sakaeo Holding Center for Cambodians I saw many children separated from their parents, afflicted with malaria and malnutrition. . . . The plight of the children is distressing. Indeed, a generation of Cambodian children is in danger of being lost.

One of the most common feelings among the Cambodian children who witnessed the mass murder of their families and friends is distrust and sometimes even hatred for the world of adults as they saw it from 1975 on. Teachers in charge of orphans in one of the camps say that several of these young boys and girls wanted to commit suicide. "We dissuaded them and did our best to help, by bringing them in contact with children in villages nearby. By joining in games and communal activities, they began to share things, both their pains and hopes."

Another camp official relates, "The most difficult task at the

CAMBODIAN CHILDREN IN THE CAMP AT SA KAEO IMPROVISE A GAME OUT OF A PIECE OF CHARCOAL AND A HANDFUL OF STONES.   (BRENDAN BEIRNE / THE SAVE THE CHILDREN FUND / U.K.)

outset was to teach them the most simple reaction: to smile."
In other places children draw their bad memories. The harsh
pencil lines and colors bring out the depths of their feelings and
seem to calm their anguish. These children have lived through
more in their first years than most of us endure in a lifetime.

Yet another camp worker says, "We are dealing here with
children who have not had a childhood. A sick or hungry child
can be cared for and fed. An injured child can be helped with
the aid of artificial legs or arms. But they haven't invented an
alternative to replace childhood."

Joel Brinkley, writing in the Louisville *Courier-Journal,* tells
the story of one Cambodian refugee:

"It is very sad about my country," said Say Khol, a 30-year-old
man who once taught English in Phnom Penh. He was sitting in
Cambodia's Samet Meanchey refugee camp a half-mile from the Thai
border, drawing in the dirt as he talked.

"Small boy, he no have anything to learn. Old man, he no have
anything to eat. Cambodia is only here. This all that is left of my
country. Soon this will be gone too."

Like many Cambodians, Say spoke English often "until Pol Pot.
Since then, I scared to speak one word or I be killed. I forget so
much."

Pol Pot is the Communist commander whose Khmer Rouge soldiers
overthrew the American-backed military government of Gen. Lon
Nol in 1975. . . . After the overthrow, Pol Pot's soldiers began exe-
cuting everyone with any hint of wealth or education—especially
those who spoke a foreign language.

The executions were supposed to purge centuries of Western influence and remake Cambodia into a self-sufficient, rural society.

Death came swiftly from machetes and bullets, or slowly from
prolonged torture. More than a million Cambodians died that first
year.

Some were hung upside down by their feet, their heads submerged
in buckets of water. They remained alive as long as their neck muscles
could hold their faces out of the water. Still others were publicly
disemboweled.

Children were chained together, then buried alive.

Say, a handsome young man, had been a lieutenant in Lon Nol's army. But when the Khmer Rouge forces approached Phnom Penh, "I threw away my uniform, put on clothes to look like an ordinary farmer and tried to leave the city."

The executions had already begun.

"I saw many, many people killed, hit on the back of the neck with a bamboo knife. They threw the bodies into huge, big piles in the middle of the street.

"I saw my friends in those piles."

He escaped the Khmer Rouge's notice. Then with the rest of Phnom Penh's survivors, he said, "I got pushed by Pol Pot into the country, to Kampong Speu Province" in southwestern Cambodia.

Like other survivors, Say was forced to live on a commune and work as a rice farmer for several years, conscious every minute that he'd be executed the moment he betrayed his middle-class past.

"They pushed me very, very hard. I worked every day, 4 A.M. to 11 P.M., with only two meals. No religious holidays."

At communes across the country, Khmer Rouge soldiers would, without warning or apparent provocation, grab workers and take them away. Sometimes weeks or months later, Say and other refugees said, workers would stumble upon mangled bodies in the corner of a rice field.

"Later, Pol Pot pushed me to Battambang Province [in western Cambodia], where we built a big, big water tank," Say said. "No machines or tools. Just people. We worked 24 hours a day, seven days a week until it was finished. Many people, old people and young people, they died, dropped while we worked, and we worked around them.

"We have only a little bit to eat. Seven spoons of rice a day. Seven spoons, sir. That's all. Sometimes we eat only salt and little animals and the leaf of a tree."

Millions of Cambodians in other communes suffered along with him. . . .

Say Khol . . . sneaked off one night this fall with the thin bandolier of rice he had saved and walked to Thailand.

"I walk five days," he said, counting on his fingers. "More than

100 kilometers. I walk at night and see many, many others walking too, some fast, some very slow.

"We dive into bushes if we see Vietnamese soldiers coming. Some of us very sick. Many, many bodies lying by the road. Everywhere it smells bad from the dead."

Now Say squats with the 200,000 others in the border encampment and waits.

"My family is alive in Battambang, and they will come soon," he says with more hope than conviction. "I know they will come."

The story of Say Kohl is typical. Through the incredible suffering of the Indochinese refugees, we can see the injustices, the oppression and maltreatment of the powerless by the powerful everywhere in the world. Their plight tests human reason and conscience. This is especially so at a time of economic uncertainty in the industrial democracies and frustration in the developing world. Refugees challenge in a particularly sharp way what we call the international community. To a very great extent, how we treat the dispossessed and the powerless is a test of our humanity.

4 · LIFE IN *Refugee* CAMPS

Refugees usually need emergency help. After the ordeal of flight from their home countries, they are hungry and often ill. Local food is scarce, and medical supplies and health care still more scarce. Water is often in short supply.

Unfortunately, refugees cannot always be seen as a purely humanitarian problem. In addition to the human side of the tragedy, there is the economic burden that refugees impose on national and local economies of receiving countries. Most of today's refugees flee from one Third World country to another. These countries are often as poor as the refugees themselves. It is difficult for them to receive, feed, clothe, and educate hundreds of thousands of newcomers when many of their own people suffer from malnutrition and disease. Moreover, the aid that comes from outside the country to assist the refugees can create tensions between local populations and the refugees. Some countries, such as Somalia, have made tremendous efforts and sacrifices to feed and accommodate the growing number of people seeking asylum. This has been possible only by seriously reducing the level of services provided to their own citizens and at the expense of the government's normal social and economic development programs. Other countries have not been so generous.

▪ Anti-Refugee Feelings

In spite of the terrors of their ordeal at sea, few Vietnamese boat people are welcome in neighboring countries. In all of Asia, from Japan in the north to Indonesia in the south, authorities have been reluctant to accept refugees. Most governments feel that they have enough economic problems of their own without taking responsibility for displaced people from other states. Poor nations themselves, Thailand, Malaysia, and Indonesia explain that they are troubled by chronic unemployment and food shortages, and that the influx of large numbers of foreigners can only increase these shortages and generate resentment against the refugees.

Southeast Asian nations resist any permanent refugee resettlement on their soil for fear of domestic instability. Thailand considers its security to be threatened by the Vietnamese-Cambodian conflict and the influx of Cambodians; while many are true refugees, others are soldiers or their families. In the face of a wave of refugees from Cambodia, Thailand has in the past forced more than 50,000 Cambodians back across the border at gunpoint. Many of these people then were starved to death or murdered. Laotian refugees in the north and northeast also pose a security threat to Thailand. In the past, some of the Laotian refugees turned their camps into bases for subversion in Laos. After resting in the Thai camps, they would filter back across the Mekong to continue their armed resistance to the Pathet Lao government.

Anti-refugee feelings run high in Southeast Asia. In Malaysia, the Vietnamese boat people, many of whom are ethnic Chinese, have aroused strong local resentment among the racially dominant Malays. In the past, Malaysian officials have called the boat people "garbage" and have threatened to shoot them. Consequently, Malaysia, like many Southeast Asian nations, has temporarily closed its ports to Vietnamese boat people. Malaysian authorities have even forced refugees trying to dock back out to sea. Most of the craft were no longer seaworthy. Supplies of water, food, and fuel had long been exhausted, and most passengers were suffering from exposure, seasickness, hunger, and thirst. To prevent the authorities from towing them out to sea, some refugees burn or scuttle their boats as soon as they land.

Under those circumstances, Asian governments have agreed to tolerate the refugees on a temporary basis. They will continue to do so only as long as the international community continues to pay massive aid bills and assume the responsibility for eventually taking the refugees away. On arrival, refugees from Indochina are kept in temporary camps and transit centers. Here refugees watch the weeks and months pass. Unwanted by their Asian hosts, they have no identification papers and are forbidden to work or travel. They are segregated from the rest of the population by barbed wire and kept under strict police supervision.

Many refugees assert that shortly after reaching camp they were robbed of whatever little they had by guards. The police sometimes kick and beat people for minor infractions of rules or for occasional escapes into towns for some diversion. The only protection refugees have against such treatment is the presence of international agencies and the force of world opinion.

The physical conditions of refugee camps vary widely, but their most important characteristics are overcrowding and lack of privacy in a restricted area where all of daily life must be conducted.

Vo Thi Tam, who told her story in Chapter 1, ended up on the tiny, storm-swept island of Pulau Bidong, about fifteen miles off the Malaysian coast. When the first 120 Vietnamese refugees were transferred to this uninhabited island in July 1978, there were absolutely no facilities. No proper toilets had been built, supply lines were not organized, storage facilities were nonexistent, and no steps had been taken to seal wells to prevent contamination of the water supply. In 1979, Pulau Bidong became the home of more than 30,000 Vietnamese refugees. Tom Hoskins and Julie Forsythe of the American Friends (Quakers) visited Pulau Bidong then and reported:

A LOCAL RED CROSS
NURSE IN MALAYSIA
FEEDS A VIETNAMESE
REFUGEE CHILD.
(NGBEH LEOW / UNHCR)

Even though we had talked with many officials we were not prepared for Bidong.

Here were the people. People clinging from rocks by the shore; people in dense long lines along the beach; people swimming, fishing, hauling water; people swarming on the dock; and people sitting, waiting. We had never seen so many people in such a small area.

These refugees were crammed into a quarter of a square mile of foreshore among coconut trees at the base of a towering hill. Their makeshift shacks resembled the homes of squatters throughout Asia. They were loosely constructed of scavanged timber, plastic sheeting, used bags, cardboard cartons, and flattened pieces of metal. The open latrines stank, especially on hot days. Everyone relied on relief shipments for survival. Everything had to be brought to the island, including food, water, and medicines. Each refugee drew a bag of rations that had to last three days, containing two pounds of rice, two packets of noodles, sugar, salt, two teabags, and a tin each of condensed milk, beans, sardines, and chicken. For most people, the diet was adequate, even if it was bland and monotonous. However, with fresh vegetables available only occasionally, vitamin deficiency was common. Thousands of refugees who came to this inhospitable island have now left. However, long after the Indochinese exodus ends, Pulau Bidong will live vividly in the minds of thousands of people.

The camps in Thailand also vary widely, especially along the Thai-Cambodian border. However, with the help of dedicated volunteers and the efforts of refugees themselves, remarkable progress has been made in turning a tragic situation into something positive. Before 1979, Sa Kaeo was a jungle clearing thirty-five kilometers (roughly twenty miles) from the Thai-Cambodian border. Suddenly, in late 1979, 30,000 Cambodians crossed the border in the darkness, sidestepping land mines and hiding behind lush undergrowth to evade Thai border guards and roving bands of Cambodian guerrillas. Anne Watts and Helen Archer were two of the first members of Save the Children Fund's medical team to reach Sa Kaeo camp for Cambodian refugees. Anne Watts tells this story:

Sa Kaeo holding centre for refugees was little more than a piece of ground with people strewn over it—30,000 of them. Hastily erected to cope with the sickest and weakest of 150,000 Cambodian people who were fleeing their tortured country, it was a horrifying place in those first few days.

There had been an unexpected fall of heavy rain the night before, turning the area into a quagmire. Hundreds of people, too weak to help themselves, had to be pulled from puddles to prevent them from drowning. At one end of the compound 10 large tents formed the temporary hospital area, each tent coping with about 150 patients. Many more lay outside waiting for help. Relief workers and volunteers were frantically coping with the gargantuan task of organising 30,000 people, many seriously ill with cerebral malaria, tuberculosis,

IN LATE 1979, 30,000 CAMBODIANS WHO CROSSED THE THAI CAMBODIAN BORDER TO SEEK REFUGE LIVED IN TEMPORARY SHELTERS AT SA KAEO CAMP UNTIL BETTER LODGINGS WERE BUILT. (K. GAUGLER / UNHCR)

dysentery and malnutrition. Roads were being bulldozed so that a daily supply of fresh water could be trucked in; latrines were being dug; cooking pots, charcoal stoves, blankets and rice were being distributed to each family. Into all this, on the fourth day after the camp was set up, Helen and I arrived. We were put to work immediately in the paediatric tent. The first two days were harrowing. Perhaps the most heartrending sight was the mothers, tearful and exhausted, clutching hollow-eyed children with death's head faces, swollen bellies, and limbs as thin and dry as fragile twigs. In the first few days 15 to 20 children a day died in that tent. Too weak and exhausted to sustain the shock of treatment, they quietly died.

On our second day at Sa Kaeo I remember clearly a woman tugging at my elbow—she wouldn't go away. With the help of an interpreter we learned that her four-year-old child had just died and that someone had removed the body. She did not know where. We found out, and took her to a grave at the back of the hospital area. In it were about eight bodies. On top lay her child. She made me take the child out. Talking to it softly, she nursed the body for a while, then placed her child back in the grave. She told us he was the last of her four children to die; her husband was also dead. Then she turned on her heel, head bowed, and walked off into the crowd.

Fortunately, conditions soon improved at Sa Kaeo. Scores of volunteers from all walks of life—housewives, students, tourists, and businessmen—answered an urgent call for help put out by the United Nations. Clinics were set up in large bamboo and thatch buildings. More permanent housing was put together by Thai labor with the help of the strongest of the refugees. Nurses and doctors attempted to see all the refugees and to refer those in most need to the hospital. Hundreds were registered, weighed, and examined. Rations of fish powder, corn, soya milk, and mung beans were handed out. According to Anne Watts: "As the weeks passed Sa Kaeo took on a different air. The health of the refugees, mental and physical, improved dramatically. They began to hope again."

Once this stage was reached, the volunteers and refugees themselves could start to plan beyond mere survival. The first step was to encourage refugees to do things for themselves. Antenatal clinics, teaching programs for native midwives and vaccination clinics were set up. The refugees started up crafts and small industries of their own. Women who had been seamstresses back in Cambodia made clothes. Men wove straw mats and rice baskets, made sandals, and carved musical instruments. Playgroups and school got started, and small vegetable gardens sprouted up throughout the camp. Sa Kaeo had been transformed from a place of misery to a place of hope.

Sa Kaeo is not typical of the many long-established camps in Thailand. Other camps have much more tolerable living conditions and have taken on the aspect of semi-permanence. The refugee camp at Nong Hai in Northeast Thailand, for example, has become a permanent city of 35,000 with wood-frame buildings, neat but dusty streets, and unending soccer games among

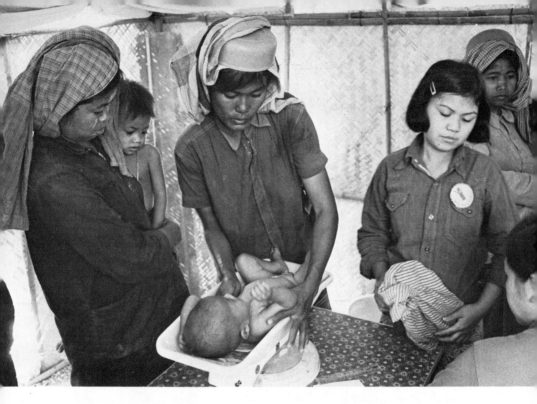

A VOLUNTEER AT THE SA KAEO CAMP CHECKS THE WEIGHT OF A CAMBODIAN BABY UNDER THE GUIDANCE OF ONE OF SAVE THE CHILDREN'S NURSES. SAVE THE CHILDREN PROVIDES SUPPLEMENTARY FEEDING AND GENERAL MOTHER AND CHILD CARE.   (BRENDAN BEIRNE / THE SAVE THE CHILDREN FUND / U.K.)

boys with nothing else to do. It has a poor but bearable subsistence economy built on United Nations relief, black-marketeering, barber shops, prostitution, and whatever else the refugees can find to do. Some refugees have endured this uncertain status for more than three years.

■ *Waiting for a New Life*

Even in camps where conditions are relatively good, many refugees undergo great psychological strain. Besides the suffering, trauma, persecution, and loss of loved ones already endured, a refugee must also deal with the loss of homeland and identity. A new life in a strange land awaits. The refugee begins to feel both incompetent and vulnerable. Anxiety, fear, frustrations, and emotional disturbances appear. Often the refugee becomes apathetic, helpless, or aggressive. Life in the camps is hard. Diets are often inadequate, and susceptibility to illness is increased. Schooling and recreation are either nonexistent or severely limited. Stress, anxiety, and confusion are a part of daily life. Many refugees live in fear of being shipped back to their country.

Women and children refugees suffer most. Many women who arrive at the camps are widows with children. They suffer from the shock of having to look after a large family with meager support in a foreign country. All the factors that make life difficult for adult refugees are more acute for children. They

AMONG THE MOST VULNERABLE REFUGEES MANY WOMEN AND CHILDREN ARRIVE IN REFUGEE CAMPS WITHOUT HUSBANDS OR FATHERS AND DEPEND ON WHATEVER RELIEF IS PROVIDED. THIS BURMESE MOTHER AND HER BABY AWAIT SUPPLEMENTARY FEEDING AT A CAMP IN BANGLADESH. (UNHCR)

are more vulnerable than adults and less able to endure the hunger, unsanitary conditions, illnesses, heat or cold, and lack of shelter and medicine.

Imagine yourself standing alone with only the clothes on your back. You are in a strange place, surrounded by thousands of people in the same miserable state as yourself. All your possessions have been left behind, and most or all of your family and friends are dead or missing. Your daily diet consists of porridge and water. If you can imagine yourself in that situation you will have some idea of how teenagers in the camps live and feel. However, life in the camps is not just a matter of material deprivation, but also a matter of not being able to plan or hope for the future the way teenagers and young people are meant to do.

The longer refugees are confined to camps, the more pronounced become their feelings of deprivation. Yet because it is cheaper to feed them in camps than in the United States or in Europe, emptying the camps in Southeast Asia is taking a very long time. Western countries will not make long-term commitments to help many of these people. Each nation hopes that some other nation will open its door. Ironically, by delaying resettlement the Western nations are destroying the very qualities that might improve the refugees' prospects for successful resettlement. Generally, the longer they stay in camps, the harder it is for them to adjust to the country in which they resettle.

■ Immigration Procedures

In trying to find a new country, most of the Indochinese refugees are subjected to lengthy and cumbersome immigration procedures. Western immigration officers examine each individual's occupational and political background, health, whereabouts of relatives, and language proficiency.

Tom Hoskins and Julie Forsythe of the American Friends spent some time listening in on the screening of Vietnamese refugees by United States officials on Pulau Bidong island:

One head of the family being interviewed was an ethnic Chinese from Kampuchea [Cambodia] whose life work was teaching (Chinese) Mandarin in Phnom Penh. They fled to Vietnam in 1975 with the rise of Pol Pot, and then left Vietnam for Malaysia in February, 1979. Their new baby was born on the refugee boat, and their question was what to do about a birth certificate.

A screening interview was with a young electronics engineer who had studied in New Zealand for five years and wished to settle there. He was advised by the interviewer that there should be no problem, except that the team from New Zealand was not expected until early June, two full months away. He had no choice but to wait for their arrival.

Another screening interview was with a former South Vietnamese sergeant who had been on the island twenty-one days, and had just completed his house and carried in a supply of water. He spoke very good English, and was vocal in his unhappiness over learning that he might have to wait six months before even being considered by U.S. immigration. He had no immediate relatives in the United States, and he had not been directly employed by the U.S. government during

THESE INDOCHINESE REFUGEES IN A TRANSIT CENTER NEAR PARIS, FRANCE, RECEIVE COUNSELING, MEDICAL TESTS, AND ADMINISTRATIVE PROCESSING. (F. HERS / UNHCR)

the war. He and perhaps four thousand other former South Vietnamese soldiers on Bidong learned that they were receiving no special privileges at this point. . . . He reluctantly planned to apply to Canada for immigration in hopes of being able to move off Bidong sooner. The long lines of those waiting to be interviewed advanced slowly: some seeking clarification, others having their hopes fulfilled, others sorely disappointed.

Applicants' papers are rarely in order. Their health is often suspect. Sometimes, although they claim to be fleeing political persecution, they are trying to escape poverty and hunger. Because refugees are unwanted, they often are only grudgingly granted asylum. If there is any chance a refugee will become a burden to the state, his or her chances of entry are poor. Few countries are willing to accept the sick, the old, or the unskilled for resettlement. Yet these are the most needy people of all.

A doctor with one leading refugee organization tells of the vulnerable refugee children who arrive in a new land alone:

In Thailand, there are tens of thousands of Cambodian orphans with no place to go. In some cases they have fled on their own; in other instances, they have been separated from their families during the transit period. . . . Organizations are quite reluctant to put these children up for adoption given the possibility that their families may be alive. Hence, unaccompanied children frequently are forbidden to depart from refugee camps.

It seems unlikely that the processing of refugees will speed up, at least in the near future. In fact, it is possible that as world attention focuses on other regions of the world, public pressure to help Indochinese refugees will diminish and fewer people will be accepted for resettlement.

■ The Worst of Its Kind

The refugees fleeing war in the Horn of Africa have not benefited from media attention to the same extent as have Indochinese refugees. According to a spokesman for a leading charity, most

INDOCHINESE REFUGEES SOMETIMES WAIT YEARS BEFORE RECEIVING PER-
MISSION TO RESETTLE IN OTHER COUNTRIES. A VIETNAMESE BOY WRITES
A FAREWELL MESSAGE ON THE WALL OF A TRANSIT CENTER IN BANGKOK,
THAILAND. (M. MUNZ / UNHCR)

of these refugees are women with young children whose husbands have been drafted into the army to fight in the Ogaden.
He says, "Children, with bellies swollen and hair turning red
from protein deficiency, make up over 50 percent of the refugee
population. Malnutrition and disease are rampant. Yet, despite
the magnitude of the problem, Somalia is receiving only limited
attention from the international community." Consequently, the
United Nations High Commissioner for Refugees has termed
the refugee situation in Somalia and neighboring Djibouti "the
worst of its kind in the world."

Part of the problem is that unlike the refugee crisis in Southeast Asia, this tragedy cannot be ended by resettlement of African refugees in Western countries. The immigration barriers
of Western nations are simply too high. Moreover, most African

refugees seek asylum in neighboring countries in the hope that one day they will be able to return home. This means that impoverished countries like Somalia, whose resources can barely support its own people, must accept massive influxes of refugees. Somalia is one of the poorest countries in the world. Although it has the longest coastline in Africa, it is incredibly dry and barren. The average Somali earns slightly more than $110 a year. Most are nomadic herders, and their only sources of income are their animals. They generally sell the animals and hides in order to buy tea, sugar, salt, and clothing. But recurring fighting with neighboring Ethiopia and drought have killed entire herds and forced thousands of nomads into refugee camps.

A spokesman for a refugee organization describes a visit to Somalia in 1980:

The refugees are housed in some thirty camps dotted over the country. They are either taken there by truck from transit camps or arrive under their own steam, sometimes with a camel carrying the household possessions on its back. As soon as possible, the women build a hut, or "aqal" as it is called, by bending over tree saplings and tying them with bark twine to make a frame which they embed in the ground. The traditional way to cover this framework is with hides and thick mats. Some families are able to bring their mats with them but those who are not able to do so have to make do with paper, thin sacking, or even just thornbush twigs which offer little protection. The basic diet of refugees in the camps is maize mixed with water, dried skimmed milk, sugar and a little oil. In some camps, not even this minimal amount of food is available.

Dr. Maureen McMullen is a physician who recently left her husband and three teenage children at home in England to work for six months in the Darbi Hore camp, in northern Somalia. She describes conditions there:

Darbi Hore is an absolutely barren area. Firewood and water are very difficult to come by, particularly as the number of the families in the camp increases. The women in our camp have to walk for several miles to find branches to cut for firewood. Generally, they tie these into neat bundles to carry home on their backs.

Water is even harder to come by than fuel. Women and children have to walk some distance to the dried-up river bed. There they dig holes a few feet deep and scrape out sand and water with whatever containers they possess. Under normal conditions, water that has been filtered through sand is pure, but once a great number of hands have dug in the same hole, the sand becomes dirty and the water polluted. Cupfuls are decanted into goatskins or jerry cans to be carried back home. Dirty water like this causes disease. Tuberculosis, malaria, dehydration, and dysentery run rampant in the camps.

These refugees are living on the brink of starvation. Somalia desperately needs massive, dependable food shipments to avert a major famine. According to Dr. McMullen, the essential tasks include: hiring or contracting engineers who will help locate

IN SOMALIA WATER IS PRECIOUS. WOMEN AND CHILDREN DIG HUGE HOLES IN THE DRIED-UP RIVERBEDS TO GET WATER. (THE SAVE THE CHILDREN FUND / U.K.)

water; improving transport and communication facilities so that food can reach the refugees more quickly; starting education and recreation programs for the large numbers of children in the camps; and training Somali health workers to administer basic health care and teach hygiene.

At present, the Somali government is stretching its meager resources to accommodate the growing number of destitute people. The United Nations has appealed for help to save the Somali refugees, and the United States and several other nations have begun shipping food, medicines, and temporary shelter. However, as a spokesman for a leading charity points out, it is often difficult to get the aid shipments to the people who need help.

Food and medicine which the West sends might arrive, for example, at the port in Mogadishu, Somalia. That port has only 4 berths. Therefore, many ships with relief supplies are forced to line up for days, waiting to dock. There is no unloading equipment. Thousands of tons of food are carried off in bags, by hand and on backs.

There are only a few warehouses. When these storage facilities fill up, food is piled near the docks. Thievery is common. The food also sometimes rots.

The refugee camps are far from Mogadishu. Roads are bad or don't exist at all. It takes days to reach the camps, assuming that trucks are available and are in good working condition.

The future is not bright for the Somali refugees. The continuing war in the Ogaden offers little hope for the eventual return home for the nomadic herdsmen. It is unlikely that these people will ever be integrated into Somalia's economy. In the meantime, the burden on the Somali government of so many refugees may become intolerable. The people of the desert regions of Somalia live in a finely tuned economic and ecological balance. Because of this, the government is concerned that vital food and energy resources will quickly be depleted by the sudden influx of people.

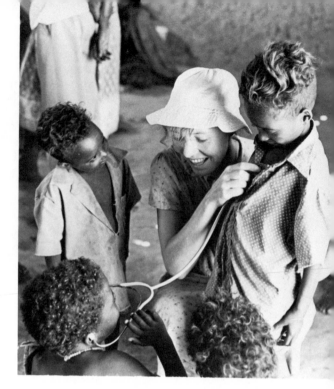

A SAVE THE CHILDREN DOCTOR SHOWS YOUNG REFUGEES IN THE AGABAR CAMP IN SOMALIA THAT A MEDICAL CHECK-UP IS NOTHING TO WORRY ABOUT. (JIM MONAHAN / THE SAVE THE CHILDREN FUND / U.K.)

■ *Search for Freedom and a Better Life*

Refugee camps are spread out not only all over Southeast Asia and Africa but on other continents as well. Since the 1956 Hungarian uprising, thousands of people have fled the Communist-bloc nations in Europe and the Soviet Union. East Europeans are attracted to the West because of its greater political freedom and higher standard of living. Most East European and Soviet Jews wishing to emigrate to the West seek refuge in nearby Austria first. In 1980 more than 5,000 refugees from thirty-five different nations passed through Traiskirchen, Austria's principal refugee reception center. In 1981 and 1982, Traiskirchen was packed with refugees from Poland who were fleeing economic hardship, the martial law crackdown, and the threat of Soviet invasion.

Traiskirchen is drab and overcrowded. It was originally an Austrian military barracks that was later used by both the Nazis and the Soviets. Inside the weathered brick buildings, twenty people often share one room. Roughly 90 percent of these East

European refugees are in their twenties and thirties, and most stay from three to nine months at Traiskirchen. All are without jobs or anything else to do. Life is difficult. Many refugees are in a state of shock and behave like robots. When the enormity of what has happened to them finally strikes home, they become depressed, angry, and confused. Among the refugees are some criminals and vagrants whom the Eastern European governments were eager to get rid of. Hence, crime and theft are prevalent in the camp. Moreover, Austrian citizens resent and distrust the refugees, and want them to return to their homes across the heavily guarded border. Most refugees insist they want to go to America, the land of opportunity, although many will finally resettle in Western Europe, Israel, and Australia.

■ Semi-Permanent Exiles

Some refugee groups have become semi-permanent exiles and have lived in refugee camps for decades. The Palestinian refugees are unique and the most extreme case of the long-term consequences of political upheaval. They now number over 1.8 million. One-third of this number live in sixty-one crowded refugee camps in Jordan, Lebanon, Syria, and the Gaza Strip. They also live in misery and despair in caves in the Israeli-occupied territory of the West Bank, in squatters' rows near large Arab cities, and in the slums of the cities themselves. Since 1948, two generations of Palestinians have been born as refugees. They still await a just settlement of the Palestine refugee problem. There seems little likelihood that peace in the region can be achieved without resolving this long-standing problem.

One Palestinian refugee child is eight-year-old Ahmed. He lives in the Baqaa refugee camp, in Jordan. His grandparents left Palestine in 1948, when the new nation of Israel was created. Like many other Palestinian children his age, Ahmed was born in the refugee camp and may have to live there all his life. His family has moved three times because of wars between Israel and its neighbors. Ahmed goes to school every day in the new

REFUGEES WHO FLED FROM PALESTINE AS A RESULT OF THE 1948 ARAB-ISRAELI WAR FOUND SHELTER AS BEST THEY COULD. SOME WERE TAKEN IN BY RELATIVES AND FRIENDS. OTHERS USED THEIR MEAGER SAVINGS TO RENT A ROOM. THE LESS FORTUNATE, LIKE THESE REFUGEES WHO TOOK SHELTER IN A CAVE IN A HILLSIDE NEAR BETHLEHEM, HAD NOWHERE TO GO.   (UNRWA)

school that was built in 1974. He hopes for a better future than that of his father, who has also lived in refugee camps since he was a child. His father never went to school, so he works only occasionally, as a laborer carrying concrete. The Baqaa refugee

THREE GENERATIONS OF
PALESTINIANS HAVE
BEEN REFUGEES. THIS
OLD WOMAN LEFT HER
HOME IN PALESTINE AS A
RESULT OF THE FIRST
ARAB-ISRAELI WAR, IN
1948. SHE SHARES A
TWO-ROOM SHELTER IN
ONE OF EIGHT REFUGEE
CAMPS IN THE GAZA
STRIP WITH HER
CHILDREN AND
GRANDCHILDREN.
(MUNIR NASR / UNRWA)

camp is overcrowded. Ahmed and his family have only one room to live in, and he has to help his mother carry their water from the tap they share with forty other families. The huts, made of asbestos and tin, are built very close together. In wet weather the dirt tracks become muddy. Ahmed and his friends often get ill during the winter, because disease spreads quickly.

During the past several years, living conditions at Baqaa camp have improved greatly, however. Although Ahmed and

OPPOSITE: DHEISHEH CAMP IS LOCATED ON A HILLSIDE SOUTH OF BETH-LEHEM, NEAR THE CHURCH OF THE NATIVITY. DURING AND AFTER THE HOSTILITIES OF 1948, ABOUT 5,000 PALESTINIAN REFUGEES TOOK SHELTER IN TENTS. LATER UNRWA, WITH THE HELP OF CONTRIBUTIONS FROM GOVERNMENTS AND INDIVIDUALS, CONSTRUCTED SMALL CON-CRETE HUTS TO REPLACE THE TENTS. (SUE HERRICK CRANMER / UNRWA)

his family have only one room to live in, additional rooms have been added to other houses. Many of the homes now have electricity for refrigerators and television sets. Some camp alleys are now paved, and camp shops offer a selection of goods appropriate for a community of 60,000.

Life in the Palestinian camps is not secure, though. Men and women teach boys and girls to fight for their people's causes, thereby inviting Israeli military retaliation. For the past several years, refugee life in Lebanon has been seriously and constantly disrupted by military raids. Between 1974 to 1976, three refugee camps in Lebanon were destroyed, one by Israeli military action and the other two by the 1976–77 civil war in Lebanon. In 1978 and 1979, and 1982, Israeli armed forces again displaced thousands of Palestine refugees in southern Lebanon and Beirut.

The 1982 Israeli military action in Lebanon was devastating for the Palestinian refugees. Tens of thousands of them were made homeless and thousands were killed. After heavy Israeli bombardment, not much was left standing in the Palestinian refugee camps. The United Nations Relief and Works Agency (UNRWA), which looks after Palestinian refugees said the Israeli attack had left "practically all the schools, clinics and installations of the agency in ruins." In addition to the repeated Israeli attacks, Lebanese Christians ruthlessly attacked Palestinian refugee camps in some areas. Marvin Howe, writing in *The New York Times* relates the story of one Palestinian woman in her sixties who was forced to flee her home in Mieh Mieh refugee camp near Sidon in Lebanon. The old woman recounts tearfully: "Some (Christian) neighbors came with armed men to the house and began beating me with iron bars and told me to get out of Mieh Mieh." Then the raiders set fire to the camp and began looting. Witnesses told of seeing gunmen firing at fleeing refugees who were silhouetted against the flames. In September 1982, an even greater atrocity occurred. Several hundred innocent Palestinian men, women, and children were massacred in Sabra and Shatila refugee camps in Beirut. Such brutalities horrify the rest of the world.

Despite these brutalities, the Palestinians have made remarkable progress. They have established businesses, hospitals,

JOBS ARE AVAILABLE FOR GRADUATES OF THE EIGHT UNRWA VOCATIONAL AND TEACHER TRAINING CENTERS. THESE MEN ATTEND THE CENTER LOCATED IN DAMASCUS, SYRIAN ARAB REPUBLIC.   (F. MAYER / UNRWA)

schools, and universities. A large proportion of their people are professionals—doctors, lawyers, teachers. Their achievements have been felt throughout Middle Eastern society, particularly in the Persian Gulf and Jordan. In general, Palestinians are among the most highly educated and accomplished people of the Arab world.

■ A New Role for the United States

In recent years, the United States has become a country of first asylum for refugees from the Caribbean and Central America. Since 1972, several thousand Haitians sailed to America, surviving a treacherous 800-mile ocean journey in tiny, overcrowded boats.

In 1980, 120,000 Cubans arrived in Florida within months, and temporary refugee camps had to be erected at military bases in Pennsylvania, Arkansas, Wisconsin, and Florida. Many Cubans had relatives in this country and quickly left the camps to join their families and get jobs. For those without relatives, immigration and resettlement took much longer. Several thousand remained in the camps for almost a whole year. These were often young single men, allegedly with criminal records, or people with physical or mental disabilities. Relief agencies found it hard to line up sponsors for these refugees.

For the first time the United States must deal with the problems and frustrations of refugee camps on its own soil. In some ways, camps in this country are no different from those in Southeast Asia or elsewhere. The camp at Fort Chaffee in Arkansas, for example, was surrounded by eleven-foot chain-link fences topped by two-foot coils of barbed wire, and was guarded by the Army and civilian police. Refugees lived in crowded barracks where there was little privacy. Their daily routine was monotonous. Many residents of the surrounding communities expressed great hostility toward the refugees and were concerned that some of the Cubans might be allowed to stay in their towns permanently.

Tensions rose to the boiling point in June 1980, when more than 17,000 refugees were crammed into the facilities at Fort Chaffee. Frustrated and extremely unhappy about the crowded conditions and slow pace of processing at the base, 1,000 Cuban refugees went on a rampage, burning buildings, breaking glass, and pelting military guards with stones. More riots followed in April 1981, when nearly 3,000 Cuban refugees still had not been resettled. In subsequent months, large numbers of Haitians, who also had been detained in camps in northern New York, Southern Florida, and Puerto Rico, rebelled against crowded and inhumane conditions.

Salvadoreans are kept in overcrowded and regimented detention centers in the American Southwest. Prison-quality food; inadequate medical care; isolation from friends, families, and attorneys; and the prospect of an indefinite and prolonged incarceration are all meant to deter the flow of further Salvado-

BECAUSE OF CROWDED AND SOMETIMES INHUMANE CONDITIONS IN THE CAMPS, TENSIONS ROSE TO THE BOILING POINT. FRUSTRATED CUBAN REFUGEES RIOTED, CONFRONTED MILITARY GUARDS WITH STICKS, AND THREW ROCKS. (JORGE RAMIREZ / U.S. CATHOLIC CONFERENCE)

reans into the United States. Rather than face this kind of existence, thousands of Salvadoreans have voluntarily signed papers permitting their summary exclusion from the United States without an asylum hearing.

In the years ahead, it is likely that the United States will continue to have to deal with refugees as more people from neighboring countries look to the United States for asylum. With the highest standard of living in the Western hemisphere and a tradition of political freedom, the United States is a magnet drawing both political refugees and economic migrants to its borders. The potential exists for new flows from Cuba and Nicaragua, sudden movements of large numbers of people fleeing state repression and conflict in El Salvador and Guatamala, and greatly increased numbers fleeing political persecution and economic deprivation in Haiti. Growing political tension and economic underdevelopment will continue to fuel large-scale migration from the Caribbean and Central America, possibly with refugees living in camps until they can be resettled.

Camp life is no long-term solution to the refugee problem. It provides only a short, transitory period of sheer survival. Fortunately, most refugees will eventually leave the camps either to return to their homes, to stay in their land of first asylum, or go to another country for resettlement. Increasing numbers of refugees are being resettled thousands of miles from home, in societies and cultures vastly different from their own. Quite naturally, this causes great anxiety for many refugees.

5 · RESETTLED Refugees

Many of the world's homeless are crossing the oceans to put down new roots in alien lands. Resettlement in distant countries is not the solution that relief officials and many refugees themselves prefer. They would rather see people repatriated to their original homes. Failing that, they would like to see uprooted people find new homes in neighboring nations with similar cultures and customs. But these are ideal solutions that are frequently impossible to achieve. Hence, relief officials try to help refugees resettle in other countries. This process creates difficulties for both refugees and those helping them.

Once refugees have settled in a new country, the real work of adapting begins. Moving to a country with a very different culture means learning everything from the beginning. They must learn how to earn a living, how to behave in the new society, to speak a new language, to like new food, to endure a different climate, and to make new friends. For refugees to adapt successfully, they must feel welcome. No one enjoys being treated as an unwelcome alien. The recent experiences of refugees may have made them especially vulnerable to insult and rejection. They need the assurance that they will enjoy the privileges and rights of citizens. They are entitled to the protection of the law, the right to work, freedom of movement, and freedom of expression.

MANY REFUGEES SETTLE THOUSANDS OF MILES FROM THEIR HOMES. THIS CHILEAN FAMILY WILL MAKE A NEW LIFE IN FRANCE (F. ZURECK / UNHCR)

■ *Resettlement in Western Nations*

There is no one single successful resettlement model used for refugees by Western countries. Every resettlement country has adopted a different approach, but the overall end goal of resettlement activities is self-sufficiency for the refugee. Basically, there are two types of resettlement procedures. Some countries prefer to keep refugees in special centers, gradually easing them into new lifestyles. France, Switzerland, and Canada, for example, have created special "adaptation" hostels to help new arrivals overcome culture shock. Help is offered through language courses, job counseling, work-training programs, housing, and education sessions. Only after several months of initiation into their new society do the refugees settle in different parts of the country. Even then, volunteer groups continue to monitor their needs.

Despite the enormous difficulties of integrating refugees into totally different cultures, resettlement for the most part seems to be working. The resettlement record for the Indochinese refugees is most impressive. By the end of 1980, more than 500,000 Indochinese had been permanently settled in the West, although tens of thousands did still remain in Southeast Asian camps. The United States heads the list of countries that have accepted the Indochinese, followed by China, France, Canada, Australia, and Germany. The remaining boat people are scattered in various other Western European countries.

One of the most comprehensive efforts to integrate the In-

REFUGEES MUST FIND WAYS TO USE THEIR SKILLS OR THEY MUST LEARN NEW ONES. LAO REFUGEES IN THAILAND DO TRADITIONAL SEWING AND EMBROIDERY. (P. JAMBOR / UNHCR)

dochinese has been made by the Australians. Upon arrival in Australia, the refugees are housed in government-run hostels for four months to a year. There they study English and attend orientation classes. Most get jobs quickly and keep them. Australian employers find the refugees exceptionally hard-working and stable.

In Europe, France's reception of refugees has been impressively warm and well organized. Because Indochina was once a French colony, France has traditionally attracted large numbers of Indochinese refugees. By the early 1970s, France had a thriving Vietnamese community. Hundreds of restaurants, shops, and small businesses in Paris, in the south of France, and in many provincial towns are run by Vietnamese. After 1975, the community was crowded with refugees fleeing the Communist takeovers in Vietnam, Cambodia, and Laos.

The newcomers to France spend their first months in resettlement centers located throughout the country. There they are provided with French language lessons, clothing, spending money, and other necessities. Jobs, however, have been hard to find in a time of economic difficulties. Even so, an estimated 80 to 90 percent of those admitted have found homes and employment.

Nevertheless, some French people criticize the government for taking in Indochinese refugees when hundreds of thousands of North African workers face expulsion because of high unemployment. Critics complain that automobile factories have hired numerous Indochinese for jobs that once were held by French workers or other immigrants. Despite these complaints, the Indochinese are being assimilated without much difficulty. Most French people consider the Indochinese good workers, reliable tenants, and polite neighbors.

Canada historically has played an active role in efforts to resettle large numbers of refugees. The Vietnamese refugees are no exception. In particular, private organizations and individuals have responded generously to the Indochinese refugee crisis. Private sponsorship groups and churches have supplied housing and other essentials. The degree of personal involvement among Canadians has given an emotional boost to the homesick refugees.

LEARNING THE LANGUAGE OF ONE'S NEW COUNTRY IS THE FIRST STEP
TOWARD LOCAL INTEGRATION. VIETNAMESE REFUGEES LEARN FRENCH IN
CANADA. (H. GLOAGUEN / VIVA / UNHCR)

■ *Resettlement in the United States*

The approach to resettlement in the United States is to encourage refugees to immerse themselves immediately in their
new society and to become self-sufficient quickly. Many volunteer agencies have carried the main load of resettling refugees
since World War II, and they try to ease the process. They also
undertake the important task of preparing local communities
for the arrival of refugees.

With the help of scores of these private voluntary agencies,
such as the U.S. Catholic Conference and the International
Rescue Committee, the United States government has helped
to resettle over 500,000 Indochinese over the last seven years.
This effort has largely been successful.

From the moment of arrival in the United States, refugees
are thrust into everyday American life, where they must cope
with a new language and an alien culture. In addition to the
trauma of escape and separation, they also experience culture

shock because of unfamiliar housing, food, and climate. The newly arrived refugees range from illiterate peasants to highly educated professionals. For all of them, life in America is difficult. Many speak little or no English and have no job skills immediately transferrable to the American labor force. Most of the Cambodians and Laotians have spent idle years in the camps. They have received no formal orientation about what it means to be a refugee in the United States. They are almost totally unprepared for Western culture or a technological society. Although the resettlement route from camps in Thailand now includes a stay in the Philippines where refugees are told about what kind of life awaits them in the U.S., they feel disoriented and frightened. In response to this situation, church groups and individuals who act as sponsors provide some social and economic security for the refugees, as well as help in finding housing, employment, and other forms of assistance from the United States government.

Despite these difficulties the Vietnamese are surviving quite well in their new environment. A study done for the U.S. Department of Health and Human Services shows that 90 percent of Vietnamese refugee households are receiving income from employment. Less than 10 percent are totally dependent on welfare. Indeed, the fact that fewer than one-quarter of the households in the United States are presently receiving any public assistance indicates that the Vietnamese are moving toward economic self-sufficiency. Early fears that they would become a financial burden for American tax-payers appear to have been unfounded.

■ Resettlement Problems

Despite the progress of the refugees, many Americans resent them. Some Americans fear that the newcomers are taking much-needed jobs away from others or are a drain on the welfare rolls. In Maine, for example, where four hundred Vietnamese settled in 1975 some unemployed young people have occasionally roughed up and robbed the Vietnamese. In the South,

American nativism has once again reared its ugly head. Recent reports state that members of the Ku Klux Klan have beaten up Vietnamese shrimp fishermen in Galveston, Texas. After being repeatedly terrorized by the Klan, over 60 percent of the Vietnamese fishermen sold their boats and left the community. In Denver, Mexican-Americans reacted violently when twenty-four Indochinese families were given apartments in a housing project that had a long waiting list of Hispanics. After rock- and bottle-throwing incidents, other housing was found for the refugees. Similar tensions are building up elsewhere in the United States, particularly in large cities, where the bulk of refugees have settled.

While the Vietnamese have encountered some public hostility, the fact that so many Americans have acted as sponsors for refugee families indicates that many Americans do welcome them. The Vietnamese have not had to deal with the severe hostility and blatant discrimination encountered by earlier Asian groups.

In many smaller communities, refugees have been praised for their industry and spirit. Today, Vietnamese refugees are welcomed by some states in America. In Iowa, for example, when Governor Robert Ray went on television to ask Iowans to "open their hearts" to the refugees from Indochina, the response was so great that Iowa quickly gained a reputation in Asian camps as a state that wanted and helped refugees. The governor of Iowa has put the power and resources of his office behind the refugees. Instead of leaving the job of resettlement to voluntary agencies, the Iowa state government gets directly involved in locating sponsors. Iowa's refugee program has been such a success that it has become a model for similar programs in Michigan, in New Jersey, and elsewhere.

It should be noted, however, that Indochinese refugees still face many problems. Regardless of the amount of assistance given to them, refugees cannot be compensated for what they have lost, nor can they be assured of a future. Whether they left their homelands on their own initiative or were forced to flee, they have cut ties with the land and people of their birth, breaking away from all they know about life. Only memories remain. Sometimes these memories are replaced by hopes for a new and better way of life, but even if the refugees' adjustment is successful, the shock of loss remains. Refugees are usually dispossessed of material things. They have also lost a personal and social heritage that can never be regained. In addition, most refugees have suffered incredible hardships from which some will never recover. The psychological problems and the sense of rootlessness will not disappear in the near future, if ever.

Many Indochinese coming to the United States, for example, are uneducated farmers who, in addition to speaking no English, are not used to city lifestyles. They often endure extreme culture shock. In 1980, a Laotian man in Iowa was so despondent that he tried to kill himself, his wife, and their three children. A son died. Wayne King of *The New York Times* recently reported the case of another Laotian refugee named Leng Vang:

> For some refugees, like 29-year-old Leng Vang, who came to Minneapolis in 1976 and whose adaptation has been conspicuously successful—two cars, house in the suburbs, good job and respect of his peers—the past can still return to haunt. In the midst of his American dream, there is a recurring nightmare.
>
> "It has to do with war," he said, "back in Laos. It is getting to be worse."
>
> "In the dream," he said, "I am in uniform and fighting, being shot, being wounded, being punished, being forced to surrender."
>
> Often, he said, there is a singular aspect to the nightmare: as he is pursued he carries an American briefcase, and wears American shoes. He tries to discard them.
>
> "I think of putting the things away from me," he said, with a small laugh, "and dressing like a H'mong villager, so I will not seem to be educated by the Americans, so I would survive."

Another major problem for the Indochinese is loneliness. Unlike other immigrant groups in America, the Indochinese who have arrived since 1975 have found no indigenous ethnic community to give them emotional or material support. Some have jobs of lower status than those they held in Indochina, and their pay is low by American standards. Others have skills that are not needed in the new society. Strains often appear at home when the husband can't provide for the family alone. The woman must work, and the children no longer respect the old ways. It is hard work even to make oneself understood at the supermarket or on the bus. Nostalgia, depression, anxiety, guilt, anger, and frustration can become so severe that many refugees toy with the idea of going home even though they fear the consequences. For many, it takes several years of uncertainty before they are sure they have made the right decision.

To counter some of these social and cultural difficulties, the Indochinese in the United States have been regrouping for the past several years. They have been moving from small towns to large metropolitan areas, forming substantial ethnic communities in such cities as Dallas, New Orleans, San Francisco, and Los Angeles. In these cohesive communities, refugees have started an increasing number of successful large and small businesses, creating jobs for themselves and others. What is most impressive is the refugees' drive to rebuild their lives and to prepare for what many hope will be a bright future. Many refugees have achieved success in the United States. For example, when Lap Huynh and his family arrived from Vietnam in 1975, they had only a few pieces of clothing. Today they own one of the San Francisco area's finest French restaurants.

One of the most difficult problems in resettling refugees is finding homes for those who have physical or mental disabilities. The difficult cases, like the handicapped, the sick, the old, the unemployable, tend to be forgotten, and they linger with growing hopelessness in camps around the world. Most countries, including the United States, are reluctant to accept these "unproductive" people. Two outstanding exceptions to this reluctance are Sweden and Switzerland. Since 1954, for example, Switzerland has resettled several thousand physically and mentally handicapped refugees from Vietnam, Hungary, Czechoslovakia, and Chile. In addition, Switzerland has also taken in 3,000 other Indochinese refugees, the majority of them disabled. In Switzerland, they receive medical treatment, language courses, job training, and other orientation.

HANDICAPPED REFUGEES ARE THE MOST DIFFICULT TO PLACE IN OTHER
COUNTRIES. THIS VIETNAMESE FAMILY OF THREE INCLUDES A RETARDED
FOUR-YEAR-OLD CHILD. SWITZERLAND, ONE OF THE FEW COUNTRIES
ACCEPTING HANDICAPPED REFUGEES, RESETTLED THIS FAMILY.
(D.A. GIULIANOTTI / UNHCR)

■ Special Problems of Children

The largest problem group of all is made up of children. More
than half of the world's refugees are under the age of sixteen.
The needs of refugee children, on any continent, in any cir-
cumstance, remain similar to the needs of children everywhere:

security, family life, food, clothing, shelter, health care, education, and a chance to compete for a viable future. Children are the ones most likely to suffer most from malnutrition, overcrowding, climatic change, and illness. What refugee children lack most of all is security and stability. In normal conditions, their parents would provide security, but this is not possible for many refugee children. All that is familiar has been left behind. It is a rare refugee family that manages to escape intact, and often only one parent survives the flight. If the family unit has managed to stay together, the parents too are deeply affected by the events that have radically changed their lives. They are unable to comfort the children with the assurance that life will be better in the future. The parents themselves view survival as paramount, and the special needs of their children may go unnoticed.

THE CHILDREN'S EDUCATION MUST NOT BE NEGLECTED. THESE YOUNG REFUGEES ATTEND AN OPEN-AIR KORANIC SCHOOL IN SOMALIA. (THE SAVE THE CHILDREN FUND / U.K.)

Many refugee children, however, are proving to be adaptable. The following story comes from the Office of the United Nations High Commissioner for Refugees. It is about Shailesh, whose parents arrived in the United States from Uganda in November 1972:

Shailesh M. stepped up to the mound and faced the batter. The pressure was on. There were two boys out, and the count was two strikes and one ball. With a motion that owed a heavy debt to his training as a cricket bowler, Shailesh pitched. The ball came in hard and fast—too fast for the batter who reacted a split second too late and struck out. Shailesh's pitching had again retired the opposing side, to the delight of the girls in the cheering section.

First as a student and now as an athlete in an unfamiliar sport, Shailesh, a displaced Asian from Uganda, was proving himself and was winning the respect and friendship of his American schoolmates.

Shailesh was one of some 40,000 Asians from Uganda who were hit by President Idi Amin's order in August 1972 expelling all Asians who did not possess Ugandan nationality. Although these persons had lived and worked in Uganda for generations, they were given just 90 days to get out of the country.

■ Traditional Roots or a New Culture

A particularly controversial question facing resettlement countries is whether to encourage refugees to abandon their native culture. Relief agencies and resettlement countries are divided. Some believe new arrivals should be totally immersed into the culture of their adopted country and made to understand that it is nonproductive to dream about a homeland to which they can never return. In the United States, for example, the emphasis is on learning American customs and English as quickly possible, even though it can provoke serious family schisms. Parents are frustrated because they are unable to adapt quickly to an alien culture. The young are fascinated by a new way of life. Without firm cultural encouragement, they can lose touch with their own traditions and become ashamed of their parents.

Other countries feel that refugees with strong cultural identities are better able to adjust to their new environments. In Switzerland, for example, there are ten scattered Tibetan communities, each with 50 to 240 members. Each group is small enough to become part of a local community, but a special effort is made to preserve the group's special culture and identity. Most Tibetans would return to their beloved mountain homeland if conditions improved and the Chinese guaranteed freedom of religion and culture. Consequently, the Swiss feel that as long as hope for a return home exists, the Tibetans should retain their cultural identity.

The French are engaged in a remarkable resettlement effort in Guyana, in South America. The H'mongs, a group of people used to living in tight-knit clans in the jungles of Laos, have fled their homes to Thailand in increasing numbers since 1975. In 1977, the French started to resettle hundreds of H'mong refugees in Guyana, where physical and socioeconomic conditions are similar to those in Laos. After much hard work in the clearing of thick jungle undergrowth, a H'mong village was created and agricultural crops planted. The experiment has proven to be remarkably successful. Some European and American relief officials believe that such projects should be expanded, particularly for refugees who are not suited to urbanized Western living.

Some observers also stress that eventual repatriation should never be ruled out. One can point to the nearly 200,000 Muslims who, after a year's absence, returned to their homes in Burma in 1979. So too were thousands of Zimbabwean refugees repatriated from the asylum countries of Botswana, Mozambique, and Zambia following a long war of national independence. Both Brazil and Bolivia have apparently succeeded in drawing thousands of refugees back to their former homelands under amnesty programs. Several hundred thousand Cambodians returned home from Thailand 1n 1981. Tibetan refugees in India, Nepal, and Europe are also contemplating a journey home if China's promises for greater autonomy and religious freedom prove genuine. Thus, to some extent, it is possible to refute the commonly held belief that refugees never return home.

The numbers of refugees in the world today are so large that

THESE BURMESE REFUGEES WERE ALLOWED TO RETURN TO THEIR HOMES ONE YEAR AFTER THEIR FLIGHT.   (J. CUENOD / UNHCR)

it is unrealistic to believe that industrialized nations will resettle them all within their own borders. Many countries receiving refugees find it increasingly difficult to absorb them. Countries like Sweden and Denmark are considered to be close to saturation. In Britain, the Netherlands, and West Germany, refugees and immigrants from southern Europe, former colonies, and developing nations sorely test the tolerance levels of their own people. Refugee policy is of special and rapidly growing political importance in the United States, where anti-refugee sentiment appears to be growing.

6 · THE UNITED STATES AND Refugees

The attitudes of the American people toward refugees have ranged from fear and mistrust to sympathy and admiration during the two hundred years that we have been a nation. The United States has two traditions: It welcomes refugees as the strangers at the gate; and it uses the foreign-born in times of crises as scapegoats for unsolved social problems.

■ Open Immigration

When our country was founded, its citizens were largely refugees or children of refugees. Since the European colonies were first established in America, an estimated fifty million men and women have made the journey to this country. They came in waves, reflecting events and conditions in the Old World. Some were driven by war, famine, or prejudice. Others were lured by tales of gold and free land. They came from every nation, from every class, and from every religious persuasion. We are a diverse people, but we share a common heritage: flight from the Old World and a fresh start in a new country.

For the first hundred years of our history, immigration to the United States was free and unrestricted. There was no distinction between immigrant and refugee. Any alien who could reach our shores was free to enter the country. The potato famine in Ireland in 1847 brought hundreds of thousands to the cities of the East Coast. The failure of the social revolution in Germany in 1848 brought many intellectuals and political radicals. All of these immigrants would today be considered refugees by some definition.

Throughout most of the nineteenth century, Americans regarded their country as a refuge for the poor people of Europe and looked to these immigrants as suppliers of much-needed population and cheap labor. Until the 1880s, almost anyone who wanted to come here could do so.

■ Restrictive Immigration

In the 1880s, the United States initiated a policy of controlled immigration and began to exclude certain categories of people. The first to be rejected were those who had certain diseases or criminal tendencies, or who would be unable to support themselves. In 1882, the first Chinese Exclusion Act was passed in response to the claim of workers in California that Chinese laborers were taking jobs away from native American workers. This law barred further immigration of Chinese into this country and prevented them from obtaining American citizenship.

For most other people, however, the gates remained open. During the 1890s and the first two decades of the twentieth century, vast numbers of immigrants from southern and eastern Europe began arriving in the United States. Grinding poverty and war drove Italians and Greeks from their homes. Pogroms in Russia and Poland brought Jews in growing numbers. Hungarians, Czechs, and Poles fled from political oppression and military conscription. Between 1900 and 1914, a record thirteen million people entered the United States as immigrants.

As the number of immigrants increased, agitation for further restriction on immigration increased. Recent arrivals had life-styles that were noticeably different from those of groups already settled in the United States. Moreover, their arrival coincided with a depression in the 1890s and with rising nationalism. Americans feared that the once-endless supply of land was running out. They were afraid that hordes of Europeans fleeing their war-torn countries would descend on the United States and change the way of life here. Speaking before Congress in 1896, Senator Henry Cabot Lodge expressed the widespread concern that the influx of these new immigrants would threaten national unity and diminish the quality of life: "The injury of unrestricted immigration to American wages and American standards of living is sufficiently plain and is bad enough but the danger which this immigration threatens to the quality of our citizenship is far worse."

Responding to the demand for restrictive immigration, Congress rejected the long-standing principle of America as an asylum for the world's needy, poor, and oppressed. In 1917, it enacted a law requiring all immigrants to pass a simple literacy test that was intended as a device to keep out the poor and uneducated. The test did not work, and so in 1921 the first of several quota laws was passed. These laws set a ceiling on the total number of immigrants who could enter the United States each year from specific countries in Europe. At the same time, the national-origins quota system attempted to maintain the ethnic balance then existing in America. Those northern and western European countries that had sent the greatest number of immigrants to America in the nineteenth century could continue to send the most new immigrants, but southern and eastern European countries that had more recently begun to send immigrants would have much lower quotas. These immigration laws were blatantly racist. They were designed to favor immigrants from northern and western Europe and limit the number of immigrants from southern and eastern Europe, many of whom were Catholic or Jewish and thought to be of inferior racial stock. The law also virtually excluded Asians and Blacks as well as the ill, the illiterate, and the impoverished from all nations.

The inscription on the base of the Statue of Liberty described an earlier immigration policy:

Give me your tired, your poor,
Your huddled masses yearning to breathe free,
The wretched refuse of your teeming shore.
Send these, the homeless, tempest tossed, to me.
I lift my lamp beside the golden door.

After 1920, the inscription applied only to the tired and poor who came from the right country, had the right color of skin, and the right religion.

During the decades between World Wars I and II, thousands of individuals facing deprivation and thousands of others fearing persecution were denied admission to the United States. Many Jews and political opponents of Fascist regimes in Germany and Italy attempted to flee to the United States, but the restrictive national quota laws allowed in only a few. Several proposals to admit larger numbers of refugees on a humanitarian basis were turned down in Congress. In one tragic incident, 937 German refugees aboard the *St. Louis* were denied entry into Cuba and the United States, and they were forced to return to Europe, where most of them eventually died during the Nazi occupation.

During World War II populations were dislocated on a massive scale. In addition to the millions of Jews sent to concentration camps, hundreds of thousands of Polish, Dutch, Danish, French, and other peoples in occupied Europe were seized and sent to work in German factories. Millions of others fled to escape the war's destruction and Nazi persecution. At the end of the war in Europe in May 1945, there were an estimated thirty million displaced persons. Many were eventually repatriated. However, one million persons, mostly survivors of concentration camps or those whose homelands had come under Communist domination, did not want, or were unable, to return home. They waited in camps in Germany, hoping for resettlement. In the United States, private voluntary agencies pressed for a change in the law to permit admission of these refugees. At last, in 1948, the Displaced Persons Act was passed, making 400,000 quota places available over a four-year period.

■ Post–World War II Immigration Policy

After World War II, pressure began to grow to liberalize American immigration laws. Despite this pressure, a new restrictive law was passed, the Immigration and Nationality Act of 1952. This law retained the national-origins quota system and continued the practice of discriminating against Asians. President Harry Truman vetoed the act but his veto was overridden. In a message that accompanied his veto, Truman argued that the maintenance of the national-origins quota system was fundamentally at variance with the goal of responding to the human needs of refugees:

> This quota system keeps out the very people we want to bring in . . . by "protecting" ourselves against being flooded by immigrants from Eastern Europe. This is fantastic. The countries of Eastern Europe . . . are . . . fenced off by barbed wire and minefields—no one passes their borders but at risk of his life. We do not need to be protected against immigrants from these countries—on the contrary we want to stretch out a helping hand to save those . . . who are brave enough to escape. . . .

Truman also argued that a potentially explosive refugee situation continued to exist seven years after the end of World War II. He predicted that the deficiencies of the quota system would continue to manifest themselves and would lead to a stopgap approach to refugee problems:

> The inadequacy of the present quota system has been demonstrated since the end of the war. . . . If the quota system remains unchanged, we shall be compelled to resort to emergency legislation again, in order to admit any substantial [number of] . . . refugees.

At a time of rising political tension between the United States and the Soviet Union, large numbers of refugees continued to leave Eastern Europe and other Communist-dominated countries during the 1950s and 1960s. For both humanitarian and political reasons, the United States admitted several hundred thousand refugees from the Eastern-bloc nations. Additional special legislation was passed to permit the admission of refugees from the Hungarian uprising, Fidel Castro's revolution in Cuba, and similar events. These laws permitted refugees to be admitted to the United States outside of ordinary immigration channels.

Finally, in 1965, a comprehensive overhaul of existing immigration laws was enacted. National-origins quotas were abolished and discriminatory restrictions on the entry of Asians to the U.S. were ended. The new law also established a system of preference categories and provided for the conditional entry of 17,400 refugees per year. To qualify for refugee status, the law required that persons be fleeing from Communist countries or from the Middle East because of persecution, and be unwilling or unable to return home.

The 1965 law was a substantial victory over the discriminatory principles of the 1952 law, but the 17,400 places allotted refugees were totally inadequate to meet world refugee demands. The United States definition of a refugee was politically motivated. It excluded large numbers of refugees fleeing non-Communist authoritarian regimes throughout Latin America, Africa, and Asia. Through special legislation the United States has generously admitted large numbers of persons fleeing Communist regimes. However, refugees from repressive non-Communist governments like Haiti, Chile, Iran under the Shah, and South Korea have not been welcomed. This inconsistency in refugee policy has been due in part to the priority in United States foreign policy given to security and political issues rather than to humanitarian concerns. Moreover, great importance is attached to the maintenance of good relations with America's allies. Receiving political refugees from a country implies some doubt about that nation's politics.

From 1965 to 1980, persecuted and homeless peoples by the hundreds of thousands looked toward the United States for ultimate refuge. Many Americans, especially the volunteer agencies and workers, responded with generosity and enthusiasm. Special legislation was again used to admit almost 700,000 refugees from Southeast Asia, Cuba, Eastern Europe, and other troubled areas between 1975 and 1980. Cities like Miami, Los Angeles, New York, and Chicago became the homes of most new refugees. Southern Florida remained a magnet for Caribbean refugees. Whole communities of Kurds settled in Nashville, Mongolians in New Jersey, and H'mong tribesmen from Laos in Denver.

■ The 1980 Refugee Act

The majority of refugees were forced to enter the United States under various special refugee programs because they were not eligible for entry under the ideological, geographic, or numerical limitations of the 1965 Immigration Act. Finally, in 1980, Congress and President Jimmy Carter approved the Refugee Act of 1980. Until the Refugee Act was signed into law on March 17, 1980, the United States had no formal policy of acceptance or resettlement of refugees.

This law establishes for the first time a coherent and comprehensive legal framework for admitting refugees to the United States and accomplishes several long-fought-for objectives related to human rights. It abolishes the refugee admission ceiling of 17,400 per year, a ceiling that was often surpassed. There are new provisions for the regular admission of greater numbers of refugees and for the admission of refugees in emergency situations as well. The new act also repeals the old definition of a refugee, which gave strong preference to persons from communist countries. Adopting the definition used by the United Nations, the act defines a refugee as a person from any part of the world who is unable or unwilling to return to his home country because of a "well-founded fear of persecution on account of race, religion, nationality, membership of a particular social group, or political opinion." It also provides for federal support of the resettlement program.

The new legislation has several deficiencies, however. Almost as soon as it became law, the Refugee Act of 1980 was severely strained by the massive influx of Cubans into south Florida in the spring of 1980. The act did not allow for emergencies like the Cuban boatlift and has no provision for such arrivals and mass requests for political asylum. As a result, the most recent arrivals from Cuba and Haiti had to be given temporary-asylum status.

Many critics maintain that despite passage of the Refugee Act of 1980, strong ideological, geographic, and racial biases are still reflected in United States refugee policies. For example, of the more than 230,000 refugees resettled in the United States during 1980, over 90 percent were from the Soviet bloc, Asian Communist nations, and Cuba. Only 2,500 were allowed in from all the rest of Latin America and Africa. In light of these statistics, the Congressional Black Caucus has made claims of racially motivated bias in the treatment of black Haitians and the masses of homeless refugees in Somalia. Many have questioned whether the fact that the Haitians are black and fleeing from a right-wing regime with which the United States government is friendly makes a difference. Sadly, it seems that it does, though the Refugee Act mandates equal treatment for all those who have "a well-founded fear of persecution." In contrast to the hospitality extended over several years to the Cubans, the Haitians have been received with hostility and the prejudgment that they were not genuine refugees. In the past, they were automatically detained in jail, with bond set at $1,000; they were denied employment authorization; and they were given cursory fifteen-minute interviews, with no attorney permitted, and immediate denial of asylum. In July 1980, Judge James Lawrence King ruled that more than 4,000 Haitians seeking asylum in the United States had been denied due process of law and equal protection of the law, and had been victims of discrimination by immigration authorities. Judge King found that the manner in which the Immigration and Naturalization Service (INS) had treated these Haitians violated the Constitution, the immigration statutes, international agreements, INS regulations, and INS operating procedures. Although he ordered an immediate halt to the deportation of Haitians, the United States continues to detain and deport Haitians.

While recognizing the need to deal with refugees from Communist countries, human rights advocates stress the humanitarian need to accept refugees from repressive non-Communist regimes as well. United States policy reflects a belief that people who want freedom from Communism are justified, but people who say they want freedom from right-wing dictatorships are only fleeing poverty. In Latin America, for example, many political refugees from right-wing regimes have fled because they were threatened with arrest, torture, and death. Yet most Latin Americans seeking asylum in the United States are refused entry because they are deemed to be fleeing for economic rather than political reasons. For example, following the military coup in Chile in 1971, a relatively small number of Chilean refugees were allowed entry into the United States. Most Chilean refugees went to neighboring Latin American or distant European countries. The United States government was afraid that granting political asylum to large numbers of Chileans would endanger America's relations with the military junta in Chile. In effect, politics mattered more than people.

■ The U. S. as an Asylum for Refugees

The character of the refugee problem is changing drastically. No longer do just individuals or small groups seek political asylum. Large groups of people are emigrating en masse. The pressures that have led to the flight and resettlement in the United States of hundreds of thousands of Cubans and Indochinese and the influx of tens of thousands of Haitians still exist. Moreover, continuing turmoil in Central America and the Caribbean is likely to produce many more refugees. Because of the civil war in El Salvador, for example, tens of thousands of people have already lost their lives. Untold numbers of Salvadorean refugees are trying to get into the United States to escape the violence at home. Growing numbers of Guatamalans, facing similar circumstances, are also leaving their country. Salvadoreans and Guatamalans, however, are not being admitted to the United States. Practically every applicant is turned down and deported. There are reports that many people have been executed upon their return to El Salvador. With no other alternative, refugees from El Salvador and Guatamala are attempting to enter the United States without documents, and they plan to stay here illegally.

The pressures on the United States for a liberal refugee and immigration policy have never been greater than they are today. The Select Commission on Immigration and Refugee Policy appointed by former President Carter has made a number of suggestions regarding existing laws, policies, and procedures governing the admission of refugees to the United States, but the problem of mass political asylum will be solved only when the United States adopts a foreign policy that will bring about real social, political, and economic reform in Third World countries. Resistance to large-scale, uncontrolled refugee admission and immigration is likely to increase among the American public. In a September 1980 poll, 91 percent supported an all-out effort to stop the illegal entry of aliens into the United States and 80 percent wanted to reduce the quotas of legal immigrants who can enter the country each year.

Whatever the number of refugees and illegal aliens, they have had an important impact on the economy, jobs, wage scales, and neighborhoods in many parts of the nation. They are changing the American landscape. For example, the United States is now the fourth largest Spanish-speaking nation in the world, and United States residents of Spanish origin are the country's fastest-growing minority. This has tremendous cultural, political, and economic implications, particularly in an area like south Florida. Prior to 1980, Miami's 600,000 Cubans made up 34 percent of that city's population. Dade County, which includes Miami, was declared a bilingual community in 1973. There are Spanish-language radio and TV stations, newspapers, stores, churches, and schools. In 1980, about 85,000 of the 125,000 Cubans who swamped the south Florida shores settled in Miami. This mass influx of Cubans severely strained the resources of the local community and stirred widespread resentment. As a result, many long-term residents are moving out of Miami. In November 1980, by a three to two margin, Dade County voters adopted an ordinance requiring all county documents and meetings to be in English only. Meanwhile, Blacks in Miami blame Hispanics for taking away jobs and aggravating the city's high unemployment rate. Many complain that they are unable to get jobs because they do not speak Spanish.

Asian immigrants are also changing the face of America. According to the 1980 census, Asians were the fastest growing United States ethnic group during the 1970s, increasing 125 percent to more than 3.5 million. Although many Asian-Americans are remarkably hard-working and successful, Indochinese refugees in particular are viewed with mixed feelings by local people. In Orange County, California, for example, more than 50,000 Vietnamese, Laotians, and Cambodians have settled since 1975. Asian immigrants have overloaded the public schools and medical facilities. They are blamed for a rise in the rate of tuberculosis and other diseases. In addition, lower-income whites, blacks, and Hispanics feel that the refugees are taking jobs and housing that would otherwise go to them. Because refugees often ate dogs and cats in their native lands, they have even been blamed whenever a family's pet disappeared.

Tensions have arisen between refugees and aliens and resident populations in other communities across the country. Newcomers are viewed as competitors for jobs, housing, food, and scarce resources. Labor groups, taxpayer lobbies, and some population and environmental groups claim that refugees and illegal aliens take jobs away from American workers. Because they are willing to work for lower pay, refugees undermine pay scales for domestic workers. They also relieve employers of any pressure to improve working conditions, pay, or job security. Many employers in the garment districts in New York, Chicago, and Los Angeles hire illegal aliens who are willing to work in sweatshop conditions. Some people also argue that newcomers are an economic burden on the taxpayer, who pays for the public services, the schools, and the welfare programs they often use. Finally, at a time when the United States should be holding population growth down to conserve natural resources, it is felt that refugees and illegal aliens contribute significantly to United States population growth.

While it is true that most refugees arrive in the United States destitute and in need of some public assistance in the beginning, refugees in the past have been quick to adapt to American life and have made remarkable contributions to American society. For instance, the United States experienced a great cultural and scientific invigoration from people who were forced to migrate from Europe in the past. Thousands of artists and scholars fled to America during and after World War II, and appeared in its theaters and on its movie screens, performed in its concert halls, and did scholarly research in its universities. Among them have been many Nobel prize winners, including the most renowned of all scientists, the late Albert Einstein. While others made contributions on a lesser scale, most refugees in the past have made good use of their hard-won freedom here.

Many refugees have achieved success in the United States. A federal study conducted for the Select Commission on Immigration and Refugee Policy recently showed that, on average, immigrants start earning more than native-born American families within ten years of arriving in the United States. At the same time, the survey shows that immigrant families pay more in taxes into the Treasury than they take out in welfare and other services. For example, in Miami, Cubans own more than 18,000 businesses. More than 3,500 are physicians, 16 are bank presidents, and 250 are bank vice-presidents. Carlos J. Arboleya, whose first job in the United States twenty years ago was in a shoe factory, is now president of the Barnett Bank of Miami.

The refugees' potential for self-fulfillment and positive contribution to society is often ignored. Many help our industrial economy function by taking low-paying jobs and doing "stoop labor" that American workers avoid. Illegal aliens in particular help consumers by providing a constant supply of cheap labor for industry and agriculture, keeping prices down. And, contrary to popular belief, refugees and illegal aliens do not appear to be a heavy burden on government social services. In fact, it is often overlooked that illegal immigrants and refugees are also taxpayers. Many refugees pay federal and state income taxes and contribute to the Social Security system. Moreover, there are increasing numbers of businesses, large and small, started by refugees that create jobs for themselves and for others, generate corporate and sales taxes, and spin off other economic benefits as well.

■ Present U. S. Immigration Policy

President Ronald Reagan has responded to the problems posed by refugees and illegal aliens by proposing a number of new immigration plans, some more restrictive than others. For example, he has ordered the U.S. Coast Guard to intercept boats carrying Haitians to the United States and to tow them back to Haiti. He has also called for strengthening the Border Patrol and fining employers who knowingly hire workers who enter the country illegally. At the same time, he has called for an experimental program to import annually 50,000 guest workers from Mexico and has offered an opportunity to illegal aliens already here to remain and eventually become United States citizens.

The Reagan administration has also taken a more aggressive approach to discourage the flow of refugees to the United States. Applicants for asylum like the Haitians are now being held in remote camps as primitive and inhumane as the internment centers that were used to house thousands of Japanese-Americans during World War II. At the same time, the United States is currently deporting hundreds of Haitians and Salvadoreans without asylum hearings. In 1981 and 1982 the United States Congress introduced several new immigration bills, including the Simpson-Mazzoli Bill, which seeks to control the number of immigrants permitted into the United States. The major issues are whether the number of entering refugees ought to be severely reduced, how to decide who is a refugee, and how to fund the resettlement of those persons we do accept as refugees.

A policy of strict enforcement of immigration laws, including expulsion of arriving Haitians and Salvadoreans, is not going to solve the refugee problem for the United States. In the long run, the only effective method of limiting refugees is to alleviate the conditions that create them. This will require a United States foreign policy that raises the issue of persecution abroad, helps to reduce the political and economic tensions leading to persecution, and takes action against nations that persist in persecuting their own citizens. In particular, the United States should promote foreign-aid programs for the poor. It should curtail military assistance that directly or indirectly strengthens the repressive capabilities of the police or armed forces of non-democratic governments. It should open lines of communication with nations that send refugees. And, to the fullest extent possible, the United States should make efforts to fund and help implement international development assistance programs, and it should share in the international burden of resettling refugees from all countries of the world.

No single issue more closely involves the ideals and heritage of this nation than refugees and immigration. How generously the United States responds to the world's needy, poor, and oppressed has long served as a measurement of the progress of American civilization.

7 · Refugees AND THE INTERNATIONAL COMMUNITY

Finding a solution to the refugee problem may seem impossible in a world like ours. Throughout history, people have fled injustice and war. The twentieth century has seen more upheavals and more people on the move from more countries than ever before.

Before the twentieth century, there was little organized international response to refugee crises. Few governments or societies seemed to care. It has been only in the past sixty years that refugees have jarred people and governments into cooperative aid programs. During this century, seventy million people in Europe alone have lost their homes or have become refugees as a result of two world wars and several major civil wars.

The presence of refugees reminds us of our global interdependence. Our sophisticated communications systems make it virtually impossible for us to ignore their plight. We watch wars from our living rooms and see pictures of people suffering—an anguished and emaciated Cambodian child; an overturned Vietnamese fishing boat; a starving Ethiopian in Djibouti; a Haitian refugee child drowned off the south Florida coast. The media bring home to us the immediate drama and tragedy of these people.

Practically every nation in the world is affected by refugees. As the problem transcends national boundaries so too does the solution. No one country can deal with large-scale flights of refugees by itself. Both individual governments and international organizations have tried to develop policies and programs to cope with the massive worldwide increase in the number of people who have lost their homes.

Historically, granting a haven to refugees has been the right of the receiving country, decided, in most cases, on the basis of its economic conditions and foreign policy. However, events in the twentieth century compel increased international consideration of refugee problems and rights.

■ History of International Relief for Refugees

The international machinery for dealing with refugees emerged primarily from the post-World War II experience with displaced Europeans. It was influenced in a less direct way by the resettlement efforts of the League of Nations in the 1920s and 1930s. The fulcrum of this machinery today is the United Nations High Commissioner for Refugees (UNHCR). The UNHCR was created in 1951 to offer legal protection to refugees so that they can return home or receive asylum, become self-supporting, and travel to new homes. The UNHCR is the first universal and permanent international institution concerned exclusively with refugees. Its high hopes were reinforced by the 1951 Convention Relating to the Status of Refugees, which spells out the rights of refugees and specifies the obligations of governments to them. More than seventy-five nations have signed this convention. In it, all signatory states agree not to send refugees home against their will, and pledge that they will take measures to provide for the refugees' security and welfare.

For thirty years the UNHCR has been providing for the victims of persecution, war, and famine. For its work in helping refugees, the UNHCR was awarded two Nobel Peace Prizes, one in 1954 and the second in 1981. In accepting the award in 1981, Poul Hartling, the head of UNHCR, stated that the Nobel Peace Prize to his office was a message to the world that "refugees must not be forgotten."

WITH TOOLS PROVIDED BY THE UNHCR REFUGEE WOMEN CULTIVATE LAND
MADE AVAILABLE BY THE GOVERNMENT OF THE HOST COUNTRY. UNHCR
TRIES TO MAKE REFUGEES SELF-SUPPORTING WHENEVER POSSIBLE. (JEAN
MOHR / UNHCR)

Although UNHCR was originally established to protect European refugees, over the years it has broadened the range of its activities to include refugees worldwide. Refugees are victims of decolonization, of age-old conflicts, and of the tensions created by development and growth. The huge increase in refugees in South Asia, Southeast Asia, and Africa has made it necessary for UNHCR to become one of the biggest of the international agencies. From a handful of employees working in a modest office with very little money in 1951, UNHCR has expanded to include a core group of civil servants totaling more than 1,000, plus many more temporary and field workers in seventy offices throughout the world, on a budget of more than $500 million.

Since it was founded, the UNHCR has helped more than

twenty million homeless people. Nevertheless, the UNHCR's action is limited because it ultimately depends on the willingness of governments to support and work with it. The greatest share of its funds come from voluntary contributions by governments, especially those of the industrial democracies of North America, Europe, and the Pacific area. Although the United States is the single largest contributor of aid for refugees, it ranks far below the Scandanavian nations in the size of its contribution per capita.

The UNHCR can function only if the governments of territories containing refugees permit it to do so. To care for refugees from Cambodia, for example, UNHCR officials must stay on good terms with both Thailand and the Communist regime installed in Cambodia by Vietnam. The UNHCR has been so

POUL HARTLING, THE UNITED NATIONS HIGH COMMISSIONER FOR REFUGEES, VISITS REFUGEE CAMPS IN THAILAND DURING A MISSION IN SOUTHEAST ASIA.   (JIM BECKET / UNHCR)

successful there that over 300,000 Cambodians returned to their homes in 1981. In some countries of Africa and Asia, however, governments have refused to acknowledge the presence of refugees inside their borders, and the United Nations could therefore do nothing for them. UNHCR officials have neither binding authority nor any means of coercion to use against unhelpful or indifferent governments.

Even while the UNHCR became the main arm of the international community in dealing with the humanitarian work of relief for refugees, there were soon cases in which it became necessary or desirable for other UN agencies to play an important role. For example, the World Food Program is enlisted everywhere. It is most notably present in Somalia, supplying cereals, dried milk, and other necessities to the refugees who swamp that arid and impoverished nation. The United Nations Children's Fund insures safety in Cameroon for those fleeing Chad's civil war. Another international refugee assistance agency of great importance is the Intergovernmental Committee on Migration (ICM). The ICM began operation in 1952 and had the task of preparing, transporting, and landing the tens of thousands of refugees who left Europe after 1950. Recently, in the tragic wake of the Vietnam war, the ICM became the main agency concerned with bringing refugees from Southeast Asia to the United States and Europe. It transported more people in 1980 than ever before in its history. In addition, two regional intergovernmental organizations are involved. The Organization of African Unity has played an increasingly important role in drawing international attention to African refugees. The Organization of American States has not yet played as active a political role with respect to refugees in the Americas, but it is considering addressing some of the issues.

■ The Role of Voluntary Agencies

A second group of refugee relief organizations are agencies that operate on a private, voluntary basis. More than two hundred such voluntary agencies support the UNHCR worldwide. These voluntary agencies do most of the work in refugee camps. Their

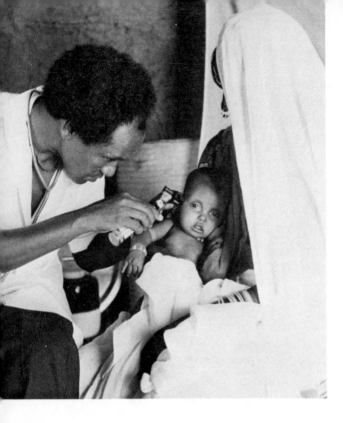

ETHIOPIAN REFUGEES RE-
CEIVE MEDICAL ASSISTANCE
AT A CAMP IN THE SUDAN.
(V. SPARRE-ULRICH / UNHCR)

tasks extend from providing simple services—such as distrib-
uting clothing—to directing vast camps in Thailand, Somalia,
the Sudan, and elsewhere. They help to find scattered family
members and counsel distraught refugees on how to rebuild
their lives.

A major task performed by nearly every voluntary agency in
this country in the last few years has been the resettlement of
refugees in the United States. While this task may be performed
by the government in other countries, it has been delegated
almost exclusively to the voluntary agencies in the United States.
The agencies give special attention to children and educational
programs, and also attend to hundreds of other needs.

The care of refugees has always been and still remains an
activity in which voluntary agencies are most effective. These
groups can appeal to the compassion of ordinary people in the
richer countries of the world. Therefore, they have been able
to mount large and sustained programs of aid, which, at times,
far exceed the resources available to the United Nations. They
can also urge national governments to react to refugee crises;

they can focus media interest on a hidden problem; they can take on the care of people whom a government may wish to "hide" for political reasons but who nevertheless may need urgent humanitarian assistance. Thus, the private agencies are a principal operating arm for UNHCR.

Some voluntary agencies make refugees their only concern. For others, refugees are only one of a number of responsibilities, which may include work in development, religious education, general relief, and health care to the impoverished and to victims of disasters. The International Committee of the Red Cross is probably the best known of the voluntary agencies, but it is certainly not the only important one. Private agencies also include giant organizations sponsored by groups in the Roman Catholic Church, the World Council of Churches, and Jewish communities. Among the more important are Oxfam, Care, Caritas, Catholic Relief Services, Medicin Sans Frontieres of France, and Save the Children Fund.

The voluntary agencies have the advantage of usually being able to ignore high-level politics. They can oversee their operations on the spot. Therefore, they can become involved in refugee situations more deeply and for longer time periods than the UNHCR. In addition, some voluntary agencies can operate in areas where the UNHCR has no mandate. Amnesty International, for example, has been helping political prisoners in Argentina and Uruguay apply for optional exile instead of continued detention. Some voluntary agencies go far beyond UNHCR's deliberately narrow definition of refugees. Man-made disasters of any kind, as well as natural disasters, provide them with their tasks. As these tasks multiply, voluntary agencies are increasingly cooperating among themselves and with the UNHCR to avoid duplication of effort and inappropriate forms of aid. Thus, in a massive relief effort such as in Thailand, more than forty voluntary agencies, together with the UN agencies and the Red Cross, make up the coordinating committee for services to refugees.

The major funding for the international refugee system comes from the governments of the industrialized countries, particularly the United States, Japan, Germany, the Scandinavian countries, Great Britain, France, Canada, and Australia. Most governments prefer to offer funding directly to the international agencies. Thus, large portions of government refugee budgets go to the UNHCR, smaller but significant portions to the ICM and Organization of African Unity, and smaller funds to private voluntary agencies.

Despite problems of coordination when dealing with vast numbers of uprooted people, the international network for refugee service works. Several million refugees—a substantial majority of those in the worst need—are helped. However, until recently this was not always the case.

■ The Evian Conference Revisited

There are few people today who remember the conference that perhaps more than any other single factor underwrote the death warrant for six million European Jews. In 1938, at Evian-les-Bains, France, a resort on the southern shore of Lake Geneva, delegates from thirty-two nations met to determine how they could rescue the German Jews from the atrocities of the Nazis. When it became clear that Hitler intended to murder all Jews in German-held territory, more and more Jews cast about for an escape from the Nazi holocaust. But country after country turned its back. Tens of thousands of refugees were turned away by other nations to be killed because of legal technicalities, red tape, and cold-hearted indifference.

In response to reports of Nazi atrocities, the world community met at the Evian conference. It was clear to all the conference participants that the Jews of Hitler's Third Reich were condemned to prison and death unless they could leave Germany and Austria. Never before in history had the nations of the world gathered together for the single purpose of saving a doomed people. *The New York Times* wrote: "It is heartbreaking to think of the queues of desperate human beings around our consulates in Vienna and other cities waiting in suspense for what happens at Evian. But the question they underline is not simply humanitarian. . . . It is a test of civilization."

Despite great hopes, the conference was a tragic failure. Delegates from one nation after another stood up to explain why their governments could not offer refuge to Jews. Lord Winterton, the British delegate, explained that an influx of Jewish refugees "might arouse anti-Semitic feeling in Great Britain." The French delegate, in eloquent phrases, pointed out that his country was in complete agreement with the principle of aiding refugees, but that unfortunately France's zeal to serve the cause of humanity was conditioned by its lack of resources. The Australian delegate, Lieutenant Colonel J. W. White, explained, "As we have no real racial problem, we are not desirous of importing one." The Latin American countries—with the exception of the Dominican Republic, which agreed to accept 100,000 refugees—stated that they had pressing unemployment problems. Most of these countries also noted that they had trade agreements with Germany and did not want to take any action that would displease Hitler and risk the loss of German trade. Even President Roosevelt's representative, Myron C. Taylor, was in no position to permit the entry of more Jews. Congress would not relax its national quota laws. Thus, the United States, the nation that for generations had offered asylum to Europe's oppressed, could hold out no hope to Jewish refugees.

The failure of the Evian Conference gave Hitler *carte blanche* to proceed with the slaughter of six million Jews in Western and Eastern Europe. In a speech made immediately after the conference, Hitler derided the rest of the world for expressing sympathy for "Jewish criminals" but remaining hard and obdurate when it came to helping them. The *Danziger Vorposten* summed up reaction in Nazi newspapers in a single sentence: "The Evian Conference serves to justify Germany's policy against Jewry."

■ *The Geneva Conference on Indochinese Refugees*

Over forty years later the international community was faced with a similar refugee crisis halfway around the globe. In 1978 and 1979 a flood of refugees left political and economic oppression in Vietnam. Many thousands went to sea in flimsy boats in hope of reaching a friendly shore. Thousands of others fled Laos and Cambodia by moving overland into neighboring Thailand. Malaysia, Thailand, Singapore, and other Southeast Asian nations confronted the international community with a peculiarly sharp challenge when they declared that their fragile societies and economics were imperiled by the influx of refugees, and that they could accept no more. Governments, voluntary agencies, and the UNHCR were all concerned. Legal questions had arisen, such as the right to asylum and rescue at sea. Immediate action and a coordinated plan were urgently needed to provide money, processing centers, and resettlement outside Southeast Asia.

In July 1979 in Geneva, sixty-five countries took part in the meeting on refugees and displaced persons in Southeast Asia called by the secretary-general of the United Nations. The United States delegate to the conference, Vice-President Walter Mondale, called upon the international community not to repeat the mistakes made at the Evian meeting. He said: "Forty-one years ago this very week, thirty-two nations of asylum convened at Evian to save the doomed Jews of Germany. At Evian, they began with high hopes, but they failed the test of civilization. The civilized world hid in the cloak of legalism."

Fortunately, a plan that met the immediate needs of the crisis emerged from the Geneva meeting. Substantial resettlement aid, totaling some $160 million, was pledged. The number of resettlement places offered by foreign governments rose from 125,000 to 260,000. A new processing center in the Philippines was planned, and international cooperation was pledged for effecting sea rescues.

Although significant positive steps were taken to alleviate the plight of existing boat people, the final results of the 1979 Geneva meeting were, at best, mixed. Relief efforts, however essential they were then, could be no substitute for trying to eliminate the root causes of the refugee problem in Indochina. For instance, although Vietnam promised to halt the exodus of refugees, no one knows whether this can be done indefinitely.

If so, it will only be by preventing those who might wish to leave from doing so. It is as much a denial of a fundamental right to make people stay as it is to force them to leave. Thus, in effect, the conference avoided the issue of human rights violations in Indochina and chose to approach the refugee problem not by reducing persecution in Vietnam, Cambodia, and Laos, but by cutting off avenues of escape.

■ Refugees and Human Rights

Today's discussion of refugees must be coupled with an examination of human rights issues. The only feasible long-term solution to refugee crises is the reduction or elimination of human rights violations. Refugees will continue to exist as long as there are persecution, war, injustice, and poor economic and social conditions. If all governments were to observe faithfully the principles proposed in the United Nations' Universal Declaration of Human Rights there would be no large-scale refugee problem. Four articles of the document are of special concern to refugees:

ARTICLE 1: All human beings are born free and equal in dignity and rights
ARTICLE 3: All persons have the right of life, liberty and security of person
ARTICLE 13: Everyone has the right to freedom and residence within the borders of each state
ARTICLE 14: Everyone has the right to seek and enjoy in other countries asylum from persecution

It is the continued denial of those rights that creates refugees today. Underlying the increase in the number of refugees all over the world is the issue of freedom and the refugees' search for a new life and a new opportunity.

While much can be done to alleviate current crises, more needs to be done to prevent those situations in the first place. Refugee crises in Indochina, Afghanistan, and the Horn of Africa present security problems that dangerously destabilize those regions and seriously threaten world peace. It is up to governments and international organizations like the United Nations, the European Parliament, the Organization of American States, and the Organization of African Unity to play more active roles in ending political conflicts. The West can also ease many difficulties in these regions by increasing development aid. Although the United States still gives by far the largest sum of money, its aid as a proportion of its gross national product is only 0.27 percent and is declining yearly. Moreover, rising inflation and other factors have decreased the real value of foreign aid to the Third World in recent years. In contrast, the world's military spending continues to increase by leaps and bounds. The world spends over $500 billion a year or about $1.5 billion per day on arms. The amount of money spent on arms in one day would solve the immediate problems of five million desperate refugees in Africa for a three-year period. The problems of refugees in developing countries cannot be solved by temporary relief. We need long-term solutions, such as economic development of Third World nations.

■ The Role of Public Opinion

Today, the UNHCR and other organizations need a way to bring pressure to bear on governments that deny citizens their rights. There are a variety of ways in which concerned individuals can actively tackle both the repression that causes refugees and the problems that subsequently beset them.

Never before have the media carried so much information about violations of human rights and attempts to protect those rights. A government can no longer hide its behavior or isolate itself from world opinion. An informed and mobilized public opinion can often protect refugees by pressuring repressive governments to change their policies. International communities— whether they consist of governments, intellectuals, scientists, or ordinary citizens—should condemn practices of repressive regimes. We need only remember that the indignant public outcry in 1979 against Malaysia and other Southeast Asian nations for turning back the boat people helped bring the action to a halt.

REFUGEES NEED OUR HELP. FOR WEEKS THESE VIETNAMESE REFUGEES ON BOARD THE *SKYLUCK* IN HONG KONG WERE NOT ALLOWED TO DISEMBARK BECAUSE THE HONG KONG AUTHORITIES REFUSED TO CARE FOR THEM. (J. BECKET / UNHCR)

Letter-writing and demonstrations can bring positive results. Even the most repressive governments are sensitive to bad publicity. No government and no political leader dares come out publicly as an opponent of human rights.

Individuals can join local refugee assistance or human rights groups. They can sponsor a refugee for settlement in their community. They can provide newly arrived refugees with jobs, clothes, language instruction, or transportation. They can urge local radio and television stations to hold refugee forums or show films on refugee problems. They can interest young people in refugee problems by organizing "refugee days" to help students realize what it means to be a refugee.

Refugees pose grave humanitarian and strategic problems, and challenge the moral conscience of the international com-

munity. Public awareness and concern are important compo-
nents in successful refugee assistance. Refugees have no political
influence. If the concerned public fails to speak up for them,
their cause will be lost. An adequate response to the world
refugee crisis requires that citizens urge their governments to
respond to the needs of refugees, support agencies providing
for their care, and open their homes and communities when
resettlement is required.

BIBLIOGRAPHY

AIUSA Refugee Handbook. New York: Amnesty International USA, 1981.

American Friends Service Committee. *Camp Experiences of Indochinese Refugees in the United States.* Mimeographed. Philadelphia, 1975.

Ashworth, Georgina. *The Boat People and the Road People.* Sunbury, England: Quartermaine, 1979.

Brown, Francis, ed. *Refugees. The Annals of the American Academy of Political and Social Science,* 203 (May 1939).

Carliner, David. *The Rights of Aliens.* New York: Avon Books, 1977.

Children. London: Amnesty International, 1979.

"Children on the Move." *UNICEF News,* Issue 106, Vol. 4, 1980.

Cirtantas, K. C. *The Refugee.* New York: Citadel Press, 1963.

Congressional Hearings on Human Rights. Subcommittee on International Organizations, U.S. House of Representatives, Washington, D.C., 1973 on.

Congressional Research Service, Library of Congress. *World Refugee Crisis: The International Community's Response.* U.S. Senate, Judiciary Committee, 96th Congress, 1st Session, August 1979.

Dimbleby, Jonathan. *The Palestinians.* London: Quartet, 1979.

Divine, Robert A. *American Immigration Policy: 1924–1952.* New Haven: Yale University Press, 1957.

D'Souza, Frances. *The Refugee Dilemma: International Recognition and Acceptance.* London: Minority Rights Group, 1980.

"East Timor." *Comment No. 31.* London: Catholic Institute for International Relations, 1981.

Forsythe, Julie, and Hoskins, Tom. *Visit to Pulau Bidong Refugee Camp.* Philadelphia: American Friends Service Committee, 1979.

Fox, James W., and Fox, Mary Anne. *Illegal Immigration: A Bibliography, 1968–1978.* Monticello, Ill.: Vance Bibliographies, 1978.

Freidman, Julian, and Wiseberg, Laurie, eds. *Teaching Human Rights.* Washington, D.C.: Human Rights Internet, 1981.

Fyson, Nance Lui, and Greenhill, Sally. *New Commonwealth Immigrants.* London: Macmillan Education, 1979.

Gershon, Karen, ed. *We Came as Children: A Collective Autobiography.* New York: Harcourt, Brace and World, 1966.

Girardet, Edward. *Refugee Crisis.* Boston: *Christian Science Monitor Reprint,* 1980.

Graham, D. L., Jr. *Illegal Immigration and the New Reform Movement.* Washington, D.C.: Federation for Immigration Reform, 1980.

Grahl-Madsen, Atle. *The Status of Refugees in International Law.* Leyden: A. W. Sijhoff, 1966.

————.*Territorial Asylum.* Stockholm: Almquist and Wiksell International, 1980.

Grant, Bruce. *The Boat People: An Age Investigation.* New York: Penguin Books, 1979.

Hanson, Christopher. "Behind the Paper Curtain: Asylum Policy Versus Asylum Practice," *New York University Review of Law and Social Change,* Winter 1978.

Harding, Richard, and Looney, John. "Problems of Southeast Asian Children in a Refugee Camp." *American Journal of Psychiatry* 134:407–411 (April 1977).

Holborn, Louise W. *Refugees: A Problem of Our Time. The Work of the United Nations High Commissioner for Refugees, 1951–1972.* 2 vols. Metuchen, N.J.: Scarecrow Press, 1975.

Holborn, Louise W. *The International Refugee Organization: A Specialized Agency of the United Nations—Its History and Work.* London: Oxford University Press, 1956.

Holland, Judith. *Caring About Refugees.* London: Christian Aid, 1979.

ICARA Report. Geneva: International Conference on Assistance to Refugees in Africa, UNHCR, quarterly.

International Migration Review. New York: Center for Migration Studies, quarterly.

International Refugee Assistance Programs. U.S. Department of State, Bureau of Public Affairs, Washington, D.C., February 21, 1980.

Kelly, Gail Paradise. *From Vietnam to American: A Chronicle of Vietnamese Immigration to the United States.* Boulder, Colo.: Westview Press, 1977.

Loescher, G. D., and Scanlan, John. "Mass Asylum and U.S. Policy in the Caribbean Basin." *The World Today*. London: The Royal Institute of International Affairs, October 1981.

Lizos, P. *Cyprus*. London: Minority Rights Group, 1976.

Marnham, Patrick. *Nomads of the Sahel*. London: Minority Rights Group, 1979.

Matchbox. New York: Amnesty International USA, quarterly.

McClellan, Grant S. *Immigrants, Refugees and U.S. Policy*. New York: H. W. Wilson (Reference Shelf series, Vol. 52, No. 6).

Migration News. Geneva: International Catholic Migration Commission, quarterly.

Morrison, Joan, and Zabusky, C. F., eds. *American Mosaic*. New York: Dutton, 1980.

Murphy, H. B. M., ed. *Flight and Resettlement*. Paris: UNESCO, 1955.

"The New Immigrants." *Newsweek,* July 7, 1980, pp. 26–31.

Newland, Kathleen. *International Migration: The Search for Work*. Washington, D.C.: Worldwatch Institute, 1979.

————.*Refugees: The New International Politics of Displacement*. Washington, D.C.: Worldwatch Institute, March 1981.

North, D. S., and Houston, M. F. *The Characteristics and Role of Illegal Aliens in the U.S. Labor Market*. Washington, D.C.: Center for Labor and Migration Studies, 1976.

North, D. S., and Wagner, J. R. *Enforcing the Immigration Law: A Review of the Options*. Washington, D.C.: Center for Labor and Migration Studies, 1980.

Norwood, Frederick A. *Strangers and Exiles: A History of Religious Refugees*. 2 vols. Nashville, Tenn.: Abingdon Press, 1969.

Patterns of Oppression. London: Amnesty International 1980.

Refugees: Africa's Challenge. London: Christian Aid, 1978.

Refugees and Human Rights Newsletter. New York: Church World Service, Immigration and Refugee Program, quarterly.

Refugees in Human Settlements. Geneva: UNHCR, 1978.

Scanlan, John, and Loescher, G. D. "Mass Asylum and Human Rights in American Foreign Policy." *Political Science Quarterly*. New York: American Academy of Political Science, Spring 1982.

Schechtman, Joseph B. *The Refugee in the World: Displacement and Integration*. New York: A. S. Barnes, 1963.

Select Commission on Immigration and Refugee Policy. *U.S. Immigration Policy and the National Interest*. Washington, D.C.: Government Printing Office, 1981.

Short, Martin. *The Kurds*. London: Minority Rights Group, 1977.

Smith, Colin. *The Palestinians*. London: Minority Rights Group, 1979.

Stein, Barry. "A Bibliography on Refugees." *News from the United Nations High Commissioner for Refugees,* Supplement to No. 4, October–November 1980.

———."Occupational Adjustment of Refugees: The Vietnamese in the United States." *International Migration Review,* 13 (Spring 1979).

———."Refugee Research Bibliography." *International Migration Review,* March 1981.

———,And Tomasi, Sylvano. "Refugees Today." *International Migration Review.* New York: Center for Migration Studies, Vol. 15, Spring–Summer 1981.

Stoessinger, John. *The Refugee and the World Community*. Minneapolis: University of Minnesota Press, 1956.

Stone, Scott, and Stone, McGowan. *Wrapped in the Wind's Shawl: Refugees of Southeast Asia and the Western World*. San Rafael, Calif.: Presidio Press, 1980.

Taft, J. V., and others. *Refugee Resettlement in the U.S.: Time for a New Focus*. Washington, D.C.: Center for Labor and Migration Studies, 1979.

Tandon, Yash. *The New Position of East Africa's Asians*. London: Minority Rights Group, 1978.

Tanton, John. *Rethinking Immigration Policy*. Washington, D.C.: Federation for Immigration Reform, 1980.

UNHCR. *A Mandate to Protect and Assist Refugees: 20 Years of Service in the Cause of Refugees*. Geneva: UNHCR, 1971.

UNHCR. News from the United Nations High Commissioner for Refugees.

UNHCR. *The Refugee Child: UNHCR Projects for Refugee Children*. Geneva: 1979.

UNHCR. *UNHCR: The Last Ten Years*. Geneva: The United Nations High Commissioner for Refugees, 1980.

U.S. Department of State. *Overview of World Refugee Situation*. Washington, D.C.: Office of the U.S. Coordinator for Refugee Affairs, March 1980.

U.S. Library of Congress, Congressional Research Service. *Refugees in the U.S.: Laws, Programs and Proposals* (by Catherine McHugh). Issue Brief No. IB77120. Washington, D.C.: Library of Congress, November 2, 1978.

Vernant, Jacques. *The Refugee in the Post-War World*. New Haven: Yale University Press, 1953.

Wain, Barry. *The Refused: The Agony of the Indochinese Refugees.* New York: Simon and Schuster, 1982.

Wilkie, Clare. *Refugees: Mirror of Our Society.* London: Christian Aid, 1978.

The World's Children. London: Save the Children Fund, monthly.

DIRECTORY OF
ORGANIZATIONS

These pages are excerpted with permission from the *1981 World Refugee Survey,* a publication of the United States Committee for Refugees.

■ *International*

INTERGOVERNMENTAL COMMITTEE FOR MIGRATION (ICM): P.O. Box 100 CH-1211 Geneva 19, Switzerland. Director: James Carlin, Regional representative: Richard Scott, Suite 2122, 60 E. 42nd St., New York, NY 10165. Tel.: 212/599-0440.

Established in 1951, arranges for processing and transportation of European, African, Latin American, and Indochinese refugees to immigration countries in cooperation with international organizations, governmental and non-governmental agencies concerned with refugees. Implementing programs of transfer of technology to developing countries.

INTERNATIONAL COMMITTEE OF THE RED CROSS (ICRC): 17, avenue de la Paix, CH-1211 Geneva, Switzerland.

Private Swiss organization that protects and helps civilian and military victims of armed conflicts worldwide. Includes medical aid, relief supplies, a tracing agency for missing persons, and a program of visitors to prisoners of war and civilian internees.

INTERNATIONAL COUNCIL OF VOLUNTARY AGENCIES (ICVA): 17, avenue de la Paix, 1202 Geneva, Switzerland. Tel.: 33 20 25. Executive Director: Anthony Kozlowski.

Independent and neutral international association of voluntary agencies established in 1962 as a permanent liaison structure for consultation and cooperation. Presently composed of 60 international and national voluntary agencies.

INTERNATIONAL DISASTER INSTITUTE: 85 Marylebone High St., London W1M 3DE. Director: Dr. Frances D'Souza.

Carries out research into all aspects of disasters including refugee communities; runs briefing and training courses for field staff, and acts as an information center. Also publishes a quarterly journal on disaster-related topics and is in the process of setting up a Refugee Information Unit.

OFFICE OF THE UNITED NATIONS HIGH COMMISSIONER FOR REFUGEES (UNHCR): Palais des Nations, 1211 Geneva 10, Switzerland. High Commissioner: Poul Hartling. Regional Office: UN Bldg., 3rd fl., New York, NY 10017. Tel.: 212/754-7600. Washington Liaison Office: UNHCR, 1785 Massachusetts Ave., NW, Washington, DC 20036. Tel.: 202/387-8546. (Liaison with U.S.)

Established in 1951 to: 1) provide international protection to refugees who fall within the scope of its Statute, and 2) seek permanent solutions for the problem of refugees. Also coordinates assistance programs for displaced persons in accordance with various subsequent General Assembly resolutions. Representation in some 60 countries.

UNITED NATIONS CHILDREN'S FUND (UNICEF): 866 UN Plaza, New York, NY 10017. Tel.: 212/754-4213. Executive Director: James Grant.

Since 1946 has cooperated with developing countries in providing child assistance programs involving nutrition, primary health care, water and sanitation, and education. Provides humanitarian assistance to emergency victims of natural and man-made disasters.

UNITED NATIONS RELIEF AND WORKS AGENCY FOR PALESTINE REFUGEES IN THE NEAR EAST (UNRWA): Vienna International Centre, Box 700, A1400, Vienna, Austria. Commissioner-General: Olof Rydbeck. New York Liaison Office: John Miles, Room 937, United Nations, New York, NY 10017. Tel.: 212/754-4214.

Since 1950 has provided assistance to some 1.8 million Palestine refugees in Jordan, the West Bank, the Gaza Strip, Lebanon and Syria. Offers basic health and relief services and education services to children up to the lower secondary level.

■ U. S. Government

DEPARTMENT OF HEALTH AND HUMAN SERVICES, OFFICE OF REFUGEE RESETTLEMENT: 330 C St., SW, Room 1229, Washington, DC 20201. Tel.: 202/245-0418.

Provides assistance to refugees after initial placement in U.S. communities, with federal funding, through existing federal programs which are administered by states.

DEPARTMENT OF JUSTICE, IMMIGRATION AND NATURALIZATION
SERVICE: 425 Eye St., NW, Washington, DC 20536. Tel.: 202/633-2000. Acting
Commissioner: David Crosland.

Administers immigration and naturalization laws relating to the admission, exclusion,
deportation and naturalization of aliens.

OFFICE OF THE UNITED STATES COORDINATOR FOR REFUGEE
AFFAIRS: Room 7526, Department of State, Washington, DC 20520. Tel.: 202/
632-3964. Refugee Program Office, Room 6313, Department of State,
Washington, DC 20520. Tel.: 202/632-5822.

Formulates policy and plans for U.S. refugee and migration programs; acts as clearinghouse
for information on refugee affairs.

SENATE JUDICIARY COMMITTEE, 132 Russell Senate Office Building,
Washington, DC 20510. Tel.: 202/224-8050. Strom Thurmond, Chairman.
Subcommittee on Immigration and Refugee Policy: Alan Simpson, Chairman.

Studies and makes recommendations on the problems of refugees; has jurisdiction over
immigration and naturalization legislation.

■ Selected U. S. Voluntary Agencies

AFGHAN COMMUNITY IN AMERICA: 139-15 95th Ave., Jamaica, NY
11346. Tel.: 212/658-3737. Chairman: Habib Mayar.

Non-profit organization that provides non-military assistance to those made needy by the
present war in Afghanistan. Solicits contributions and gifts of any kind toward that end.

AFGHANISTAN RELIEF COMMITTEE, INC.: 345 Park Ave., Suite 4100,
New York, NY 10022. Tel.: 212/344-6616. President: Gordon A. Thomas.

Provides charitable, educational, humanitarian and benevolent assistance to the people of
Afghanistan wherever they are located, either directly or through organizations with similar
purposes. Solicits funds and in-kind donations for this purpose.

AFRICARE, INC.: 1601 Connecticut Ave., NW, Room 600, Washington, DC
20009. Tel.: 202/462-3614. Executive director: C. Payne Lucas.

Private, non-profit organization with more than 30 development assistance projects in
Africa, including providing hospital equipment and supplies in Somalia and support for a
refugee settlement in Zambia.

AID FOR AFGHAN REFUGEES (AFAR): 1052 Oak St., San Francisco, CA
94117. Tel.: 415/863-1450.

A group of Americans and Afghans organized as a non-profit apolitical organization to raise
money for Afghan refugees in Pakistan, and to raise the awareness of Americans about the
Afghan refugee situation.

AMERICAN BAR ASSOCIATION INDOCHINESE REFUGEE LEGAL
ASSISTANCE PROGRAM: 800/334-0074. (In North Carolina, call 919/684-6418,
not toll-free).

Offers reliable, basic legal advice to Indochinese refugees.

THE AMERICAN COUNCIL FOR JUDAISM PHILANTHROPIC FUND: 386 Park Avenue South, New York, NY 10016. Tel.: 212/684-1525. Executive Secretary: Mrs. Carolyn Kinsman.

Provides relief and resettlement services to Jewish refugees in Europe and the United States through programs administered by the International Rescue Committee.

(R) AMERICAN COUNCIL FOR NATIONALITIES SERVICE: 20 W. 40th St., New York, NY 10018. Tel.: 212/398-9142. Executive Director: Wells C. Klein.

ACNS and its member agencies assist immigrants, refugees, and the foreign born in adjusting to American society, and work for the acceptance of all citizens as equal participants in American life. Since 1975, actively engaged in the resettlement of refugees including Indochinese, Cubans, and Ethiopians.

AMERICAN COUNCIL OF VOLUNTARY AGENCIES FOR FOREIGN SERVICE, INC.,: 200 Park Avenue South, New York, NY 10003. Tel.: 212/777-8210. Executive Director: Leon O. Marion.

Established in 1943 to provide a means for consultation, coordination and planning to assure the maximum effective use of contributions of the American community for the assistance of people overseas. A Committee on Migration and Refugee Affairs coordinates, plans, and activates for refugees assistance at home and abroad.

AMERICAN FRIENDS SERVICE COMMITTEE: 1501 Cherry St., Philadelphia, PA 19102. Tel.: 215/241-7000. Executive Secretary: Asia Bennett.

Quaker organization dedicated to humanitarian service. Provides food, shelter and supplies, especially in response to needs created by war, disaster, gross violations of human rights, where provision of relief may lead to constructive community development.

(R) AMERICAN FUND FOR CZECHOSLOVAK REFUGEES: 1790 Broadway, Room 710, New York, NY 10019. Tel.: 212/265-1919. President: Dr. Jan Papanek.

AFCR was organized in 1948 to help resettle Czechoslovakian, Central and Eastern European refugees. Since 1975, AFCR has been participating in the resettlement of Indochinese refugees.

AMERICAN IMMIGRATION AND CITIZENSHIP CONFERENCE: 20 W. 40th St., 1st Floor, New York, NY 10018. Tel.: 212/221-6751. Executive Director: Gladys E. Alesi.

Coordinating agency for voluntary agencies interested in promoting a non-discriminatory immigration policy. Acts as a clearing house for information, stimulates studies and conferences on immigration and refugees, and provides the means for joint action by its members.

AMERICAN JEWISH JOINT DISTRIBUTION COMMITTEE, INC.: 60 E. 42nd St., New York, NY 10017. Tel.: 212/687-6200. President: Donald M. Robinson.

Assists Jewish emigrants from eastern Europe through all phases of resettlement, including relief in transit, cultural and religious aid and reconstruction aid.

AMERICAN NATIONAL RED CROSS: 17th and D Streets, NW, Washington, DC 20006. Tel.: 202/737-8300.

Assists refugees in cooperation with other National Red Cross Societies, the International Committee of the Red Cross and the league of Red Cross Societies. Provides funds, supplies and assistance of qualified specialized staff in refugee relief. Reunites refugees with their relatives in the U.S. and maintains an international foreign location inquiry service to help refugees locate missing family members.

AMERICAN NEAR EAST REFUGEE AID: 1522 K St., NW, #202, Washington, DC 20005. Tel.: 202/347-2558. President: Dr. Peter Gubser.

Non-profit, charitable organization working to increase total assistance in cash and kind from Americans to Palestinian refugees and other needy individuals in the Arab world. Seeks to increase American understanding of the plight of the Palestinians. Efforts directed toward social and economic development in the occupied West Bank and Gaza Strip.

AMERICAN ORT (ORGANIZATION FOR REHABILITATION THROUGH TRAINING) FEDERATION: 817 Broadway, New York, NY 10003. Tel.: 212/677-4400. Executive Vice President: Donald H. Klein.

Founded 1922. Organizes and maintains programs providing vocational education and training for youth and adult Jewish transmigrants. Affiliated with the World ORT Union.

AMERICAN REFUGEE COMMITTEE: 310 Fourth Ave. South, Room 410, Minneapolis, MN 55415. Tel.: 612/332-5365. National Director: Stanley B. Breen.

Works with Indochinese refugees both in the U.S. and in refugee camps in Southeast Asia Medical teams to refugee camps in Thailand. Participates in resettlement of Indochinese.

(R) BUDDHIST COUNCIL FOR REFUGEE RESCUE AND RESETTLEMENT: City of 10,000 Buddhas, Box 217, Talmage, CA 95481. Tel.: 707/468-9155. Executive Co-Director: David Rounds.

Voluntary agency, composed of Buddhist organizations and Asian-American civic associations in the U.S., which resettles Indochinese refugees. Operates an English language and acculturation training program for newly arrived refugees.

CARE: 660 First Ave., New York, NY 10016. Tel.: 212/686-3110. Executive Director: Dr. Philip Johnson.

In addition to regular feeding and self-help programs in 35 developing countries, aids refugees by providing emergency supplies and the means for reconstruction and rehabilitation. This includes food, medicine and medical supplies, seed, tools, water pumps, vocational training and materials, clothing, blankets and cooking utensils.

CATHOLIC RELIEF SERVICES—U.S.C.C. (CRS): 1011 First Ave., New York, NY 10022. Tel.: 212/838-4700. Executive Director: Most Rev. Edwin B. Broderick, D.D.

Founded in 1943 under the sponsorship of the Catholic Bishops of the United States. Cooperates with local social welfare agencies in over 60 countries to provide emergency and disaster relief, refugee resettlement and rehabilitation, support for the disabled and infirm and self-help development projects.

(R) CHURCH WORLD SERVICE: 475 Riverside Dr., New York, NY 10115. Immigration and Refugee Program. Tel.: 212/870-2164. Executive Director: Dale Dehaan.

Relief and development arm of the National Council of Churches. Assists refugees in their own country as well as countries of first asylum and works closely with regional ecumenical colleague agencies, including the World Council of Churches.

DIRECT RELIEF FOUNDATION: 404 E. Carrillo St., Santa Barbara, CA 93101. Tel.: 805/966-9149. Executive Director: Dennis G. Karzag.

Receives and donates contributions of pharmaceuticals, medical supplies and equipment to assist victims of natural and man-made disasters. Recruits, screens and arranges overseas assignments for volunteer doctors, nurses and related personnel in Africa, Asia, Latin America, and the Middle East.

ERITREAN RELIEF COMMITTEE, INC.: P.O. Box 1180, New York, NY 10017. Tel.: 212/866-4293.

Coordinates relief efforts in North America for Eritrean refugees.

HADASSAH: THE WOMEN'S ZIONIST ORGANIZATION OF AMERICA, INC.: 50 W. 58th St., New York, NY 10019. Tel.: 212/355-7900. Executive Director: Aline Kaplan.

Maintains medical facilities, immigrant camps, schools and agricultural settlements, and encourages and supports medical education in Israel. Assists in immigration and resettlement in Israel of Jewish children and youth. Founded 1912.

(R) HIAS (HEBREW IMMIGRANT AID SOCIETY, INC.) WORLD HEADQUARTERS: 200 Park Avenue South, New York, NY 10003. Tel.: 212/674-6800. Executive Vice President: Leonard Seidenman.

Assists Jewish refugees and migrants from Eastern Europe, the Middle East, North Africa and elsewhere. Global network of offices and affiliated organizations in 47 countries on six continents. Provides for pre-migration planning, visa documentation, reception, transport, and other services.

HOLT INTERNATIONAL CHILDREN'S SERVICES, INC.: 1195 City View, Box 2880, Eugene, OR 97402. Tel.: 503/687-2202. Executive Director: David H. Kim.

Provides care for unaccompanied minors through its sister organization, Holt Sahathai Foundation, in two Khmer refugee holding centers in Thailand. Plans to open an Indochinese Refugee Cultural and Service Center in Eugene, Oregon for refugees, sponsors, and service agencies.

INTERNATIONAL CHRISTIAN AID: 800 Colorado Blvd., Los Angeles, CA 90041. Tel.: 213/254-4371. President: Joe Bass.

Aids refugees and displaced persons with food, clothing, special training, self-help programs and emergency disaster aid. Currently assists refugees from Cambodia, Laos, Vietnam, Afghanistan, Ethiopia, Mozambique and Angola.

INDOCHINA REFUGEE ACTION CENTER (IRAC): 1025 15th St., NW—Suite 700, Washington, DC 20005. Tel.: 202/347-8903. Director: Jesse Bunch.

Provides technical assistance to refugee self-help groups and community service providers, and information services to persons and programs involved in resettlement.

(R) INTERNATIONAL RESCUE COMMITTEE: 386 Park Avenue South, New York, NY 10016. Tel.: 212/679-0010. Executive Director: Charles Sternberg.

Nonsectarian, nonpartisan voluntary agency providing relief and resettlement services for refugees and displaced victims of war.

INTERNATIONAL SOCIAL SERVICE, AMERICAN BRANCH: 291 Broadway, 11th Floor, New York, NY 10007. Tel.: 212/964-7550. Executive Director: Mary Jane Fales.

Part of a global network of professional services for individuals and families with problems related to intercountry movement of migration. Conducts research, provides training, consultation and information on international concerns.

(R) LUTHERAN IMMIGRATION & REFUGEE SERVICE/LUTHERAN COUNCIL IN THE U.S.A.: 360 Park Avenue South, New York, NY 10010. Tel.: 212/532-6350. Director: Ingrid Walter.

Provides immigration and resettlement assistance to refugees on behalf of cooperating Lutheran churches in the U.S.

LUTHERAN WORLD RELIEF: 360 Park Avenue South, New York, NY 10010. Tel.: 212/532-6350. Executive Director: Dr. Bernard A. Confer.

Serves as overseas aid and development agency to assist with emergency and long-term help for people in Asia, Africa and Latin America. Refugee assistance is frequently channeled through programs of Lutheran World Federation.

MAP INTERNATIONAL: 327 W. Gunderson Dr., Wheaton, IL 60187. Tel.: 312/653-6010. President: Larry E. Dixon.

Christian world health and development organization which provides supplies to hospitals and clinics in developing countries. Also provides training, consultation and referral to church-related development agencies.

MENNONITE CENTRAL COMMITTEE: 21 S. 12th St., Akron, PA 17501. Tel.: 717/859-1151. Executive Secretary: William Snyder.

Cooperative relief and service agency for 17 Mennonite and Brethren in Christ groups. Provides material aid to refugees from man-made and natural disasters. Arranges resettlement for refugees in the U.S. and Canada.

MIGRATION AND REFUGEE SERVICES (M.R.S.): United States Catholic Conference: 1312 Massachusetts Avenue, NW, Washington, DC 20005. Tel.: 202/659-6618. Executive Director: John McCarthy.

Responsible for all immigrant, migrant and refugee activities conducted at the national level by the Catholic Church of the United States. Coordinates with agencies in public and private sectors in resettlement and assimilation of individuals and families in American society.

NATIONAL COUNCIL FOR INTERNATIONAL HEALTH: 2121 Virginia Ave., NW, Suite 303, Washington, DC 20037. Tel.: 202/298-5901. Executive Director: Dr. Russell E. Morgan, Jr.

Promotes cooperation and encourages communication among the many individuals, agencies and organizations, both public and private, working in international health. Facilitates the coordination of U.S. international health activities and refugee relief programs.

OXFAM AMERICA: 302 Columbus Ave., Boston, MA 02116. Tel.: 617/247-3304. Executive Director: Joe Short.

Funds projects in Africa, Asia and Latin America designed to increase self-reliance and promote lasting economic and social development.

RAV TOV: 125 Heyward St., Brooklyn, NY 11236. Tel.: 212/875-8300. Executive Director: Rabbi David Niederman.

Since 1973 has assisted Russian and eastern European refugees through all phases of resettlement, including ESL training, employment counseling, and general maintenance and health services.

THE SALVATION ARMY WORLD SERVICE OFFICE (SAWSO): 1025 Vermont Ave., NW, Washington, DC 20005. Tel.: 202/833-5646. National Secretary: Lt. Colonel Ernest A. Miller.

Provides relief and assistance within its capabilities to refugees anywhere in the world.

SAVE THE CHILDREN FEDERATION: 54 Wilton Rd., Westport, CT 06880. Tel.: 203/226-7272. President: David L. Guyer.

Provides humanitarian aid with emphasis on self-help refugee participation. Offers English as Second Language and cultural orientation programs in Indonesia and Thailand.

SPANISH REFUGEE AID, INC.: 80 E. 11th St., Rm. 412, New York, NY 10003 Tel.: 212/674-7451. Director: Nancy Macdonald.

Founded in 1953 to aid refugees of the Spanish Civil War, thirty thousand of whom remain in France. Provides economic and moral aid to the old and sick.

(R) TOLSTOY FOUNDATION, INC.: 250 W. 57th St., Suite 1101, New York, NY 10107. Tel.: 212/247-2922. Executive Director: Teymuraz Bagration.

Founded in 1939 to assist Russian refugees. Scope has broadened to assist other refugees. Has a cultural center and field and regional offices in the U.S., operational offices in Europe and Latin America, and correspondents in the Middle East.

UNITED LITHUANIAN RELIEF FUND OF AMERICA, INC.: National Headquarters: 2558 W. 69th St., Chicago, IL 60629.

Founded in 1944; ULRF grants refugee aid, immigrant assistance, educational aid, social welfare to the sick and needy; non-sectarian, non-profit organization.

UNITED STATES COMMITTEE FOR REFUGEES: 20 W. 40th St., New York, NY 10018. Tel.: 212/398-9142. Executive Director: Wells C. Klein.

Private, non-profit organization serving as a non-governmental focal point for information and education activities on behalf of the world refugee situation. Supports UN specialized agencies working to alleviate world refugee problems and monitors legislation in Congress. Affiliated with American Council for Nationalities Service (ACNS).

U.S. COMMITTEE FOR UNICEF: 331 E. 38th St., New York, NY 10016. Tel.: 212/686-5522. President: C. Lloyd Bailey.

Established in 1947; informs Americans about UNICEF's efforts to meet the needs of the developing world's children, and raises funds for UNICEF through greeting card sales, group fund-raising events, direct contributions, and special events.

(R) WORLD RELIEF REFUGEE SERVICES: National Association of Evangelicals, P.O. Box WRC, Nyack, NY 10960. Tel.: 914/353-1444. Vice-President: T. G. Mangham.

132

Assists churches, community groups, and individual Christian families who wish to sponsor Indochinese refugees.

WORLD VISION INTERNATIONAL: 919 W. Huntington Dr., Monrovia, CA 91016. Tel.: 213/357-7979. President: Dr. Stan Mooneyham.

Active in Asia, Africa, and Latin America, providing food, health care programs, medical supplies and farming equipment.

(R) YMCA REFUGEE RESETTLEMENT SERVICES: 101 N. Wacker Drive, Chicago, IL 60606. Director: Boris Kazimoff. (New York Office: 291 Broadway, New York, NY 10007. Tel.: 212/374-2285. Associate Director: Ray E. Day.)

Directs national YMCA services for refugees. Acts as liaison for local YMCAs, cooperates with other national voluntary agencies and appropriate government agencies.

SOURCES OF INFORMATION ON REFUGEES

Further information about the world refugee situation may be had from: U.S. COMMITTEE FOR REFUGEES, 20 West 40th St., New York, N.Y. 10018, or from one of the following local agencies, which are affiliated with the American Council for Nationalities Service:

ALBANY
Albany International Center
Wellington Hotel—Room 202
136 State Street
Albany, New York 12207

AKRON
International Institute
207 East Tallmadge Avenue
Akron, Ohio 44310

BINGHAMTON
American Civic Association
131 Front Street
Binghamton, New York 13905

BOSTON
International Institute of Boston
287 Commonwealth Avenue
Boston, Massachusetts 02115

BRIDGEPORT
International Institute of Connecticut
480 East Washington Avenue
Bridgeport, Connecticut 06608

BUFFALO
International Institute of Buffalo
864 Delaware Avenue
Buffalo, New York 14209

CHICAGO
Travelers Aid Society of Metropolitan
Chicago—Immigrant's Service League
327 South LaSalle Street
Chicago, Illinois 60604

CINCINNATI
Traveler's Aid-Int'l. Inst. of Cincinnati
700 Walnut Street
Cincinnati, Ohio 45202

CLEVELAND
The Nationalities Service Center
1001 Huron Road
Cleveland, Ohio 44115

DETROIT
International Institute of Met. Detroit
111 East Kirby Avenue
Detroit, Michigan 48202

ERIE
International Institute
457 East 6th Street
Erie, Pennsylvania 16507

FLINT
International Institute
515 Stevens Street
Flint, Michigan 48502

FRESNO
Fresno Community Council
325 Crocker Bank Bldg.
Fresno, California 93721

International Institute of Fresno
847 Waterman Street
Fresno, California 93706

GARY
International Institute of Northwest
Indiana, Inc.
4433 Broadway
Gary, Indiana 46409

HONOLULU
Hawaii Refugee Resettlement
Organization
(formerly VIVA-II)
100 N. Beretania Street, Room 201A
Honolulu, Hawaii 96819

JERSEY CITY
International Institute of Jersey City
880 Bergen Avenue
Jersey City, New Jersey 07306

LAWRENCE
International Institute of Greater
Lawrence, Inc.
454 Canal Street
Lawrence, Massachusetts 01840

LOS ANGELES
International Institute of Los Angeles
435 South Boyle Avenue
Los Angeles, California 90033

LOWELL
International Institute of Lowell
79 High Street
Lowell, Massachusetts 01852

MANCHESTER
International Center, Inc.
99 Hanover Street
Manchester, New Hampshire 03105

MIAMI
ACNS Field Office
121 S.E. First Street
Miami, Florida 33131

MILWAUKEE
International Institute of Milwaukee
County
2810 West Highland Boulevard
Milwaukee, Wisconsin 53208

OAKLAND
International Institute of East Bay
297 Lee Street
Oakland, California 94610

PHILADELPHIA
Nationalities Service Center of
Philadelphia
1300 Spruce Street
Philadelphia, Pennsylvania 19107

PROVIDENCE
International Institute
421 Elmwood Avenue
Providence, Rhode Island 02907

ST. LOUIS
International Institute
3800 Park Avenue
St. Louis, Missouri 63110

ST. PAUL
International Institute of Minnesota
1694 Como Avenue
St. Paul, Minnesota 55108

SAN FRANCISCO
International Institute of San Francisco
2209 Van Ness Avenue
San Francisco, California 94109

SAN JOSE
ACNS Field Office
999 Newhall Street
San Jose, California 95126

SANTA ROSA
Indochinese American Council
921 Piner Road
Santa Rosa, California 95401

TOLEDO
International Institute of Toledo
2040 Scottwood Avenue
Toledo, Ohio 43620

WASHINGTON, D.C.
Buddhist Social Service Organization
5401 16th Street, N.W.
Washington, D.C. 20011

YOUNGSTOWN
International Institute of Youngstown
661 Wick Avenue
Youngstown, Ohio 44502

INDEX

Cambodia, 26, 46, 61, 80, 109, 115
  invaded by Vietman (1978), 27
  murders by Pol Pot's Khmer Rouge
    in, 27, 28, 48, 49
  refugees from, 46–47, 52, 55, 56, 82,
    101, 108, 114
  Say Khol's story of terror in, 48–50
Cameroon, 109
Canaan, Israelite refugees in (thirteenth
  century B.C.), 8
Canada, 112
  resettled refugees in, 78, 79, 80
Care, 111
Caribbean, refugees from, 19, 39, 73,
  76, 97. 99
Caritas, 111
Carter, Jimmy, 97, 100
Carter, Rosalynn, 46
  quoted, 47
Castro, Fidel, 39, 96
Catholic Conference, U.S., 81
Catholic Relief Services, 111
Central America
  refugees from, 73, 76, 99
  repressive regimes in, 35, 36–38
  See also Latin America
Chad, 109
Child refugees, 9–13, 46–48, 59–60,
  62, 63, 68–70, 86–88
Chile, 96, 99
  military coup in (1971), 35–36, 99
  refugees from, 85, 99
China, 1, 9, 79, 89
  invaded by Japan (1931), 14
  Vietnam attacked by (1979), 27
Chinese Exclusion Act (1882), 92
Coast Guard, U.S., 103
Commonwealth, British, 15
Communist rule in Eastern Europe, 16,
  42
  and difficulty of emigration from, 42
  refugees from, 67, 68, 95
Concentration camps, Nazi, 9, 10, 14,
  94
Congressional Black Caucus, 98
Convention Relating to the Status of
  Refugees (1951), 106

Cuba, 94
  refugees from, 21, 39, 74, 96, 97, 98,
    99, 100
Culture shock, 78, 81–82, 84
Cyprus, 33
Czechoslovakia, 92
  crisis in, and Soviet Union (1968), 16
  and Nazis, 12
  refugees from, in Switzerland, 85

Danziger Vorposten, 113
Darbi Hore refugee camp (Somalia),
  64–66
Davico, Leon, quoted, 22–23
Denmark, 90
Dheisheh refugee camp (south of
  Bethlehem), 70–71
Directory of Organizations, 127–135
Displaced persons, after World War II,
  15–16, 94
Displaced Persons Act (1948), 94
Djibouti, 21, 22, 63
Dominican Republic, at Evian
  Conference (1938), 113
Drought in East Africa, 22
Duvalier, François ("Papa Doc"), 39
Duvalier, Jean Claude ("Baby Doc"),
  39, 41

East Africa
  as drought-prone area, 22
  Indians in, 18
  refugee camps in, 21–22
East Pakistan, Bengalis of, 32, 33
East Timor, famine in, 28–30
Eastern Europe, Communist rule in.
  See Communist rule in Eastern
  Europe
Egypt, ancient, and Israelites, 8
Einstein, Albert, 102
El Salvador, 35, 76
  civil war in, 99
  refugees from, 74–75, 100
  repression by right-wing government
    of, 37–38
England. See Great Britain
Equatorial Guinea, 25

Eritrea, 21
Ethiopia, 22, 64
  invaded by Italy, 13
  and war in Ogaden region, 21, 63,
    66
European Parliament, 116
Evian Conference (1938), 112–113, 114

Forsythe, Julie, 53, 60
  quoted, 54, 60–62
France, 111, 112
  at Evian Conference (1938), 113
  Jewish refugee children in, before
    World War II, 11
  and Nazis, 12
  resettled refugees from Indochina in,
    78, 79, 80
  Spanish refugees in (1930s), 13
  withdrawal of, as colonial power, 18
Franco, Francisco, 13
Fretilin (Timorese guerrilla movement),
  29

Gaza Strip, Palestinians in, 68, 70
Geneva Conference on Indochinese
    Refugees (1979), 113–115
  issue of human rights violations
    avoided by, 115
Germany
  and dislocated populations during
    World War II, 94
  failure of social revolution in (1848),
    92
  Nazi concentration camps in, 9, 10,
    14, 94
  Poland invaded by, 12–13
  surrender of, in World War II
    (1945), 15
  See also Hitler, Adolf; West
    Germany
Gestapo, 12
Ghana, Hausas in, 18
Great Britain, 90, 112
  at Evian Conference (1938), 113
  and Japan, before World War II, 14
  Jewish refugee children in, before
    World War II, 10, 11, 12

withdrawal of, as colonial power, 18
Greco-Turkish war (1921–22), 9
Greece, 9
  immigrants from, in United States,
    92
Greek refugees from Asia Minor, 9
Guatemala, 35, 76, 99, 100
Guyana, 89

Haiti, 76, 103
  and account by Menzious, 41
  refugees from, 39, 40, 42, 73, 74, 96,
    98, 99, 103
  Ton Ton Macoutes in, 39, 40
Hartling, Poul, 106, 108
Helsinki Accords, 42
Hitler, Adolf, 9, 13, 113
  program of, to annihilate Jews, 9,
    10, 14, 112, 113
H'mong (Laotian) refugees, 28, 46
  in Guyana, 89
  in United States, 97
  See also Laos
Holland. See Netherlands
Honan Province (China), 14
Honduras, 38
Horn of Africa, 21, 22, 23, 62, 115
Hoskins, Tom, 53, 60
  quoted, 54, 60–62
Howe, Marvin, 72
Human rights of refugees, 42, 115–116
Hungary
  refugees from, in United States, 95
  refugees from, in Switzerland, 85
  uprising in (1956), 16, 67, 96

Immigration Act (1965), 96, 97
Immigration and Nationality Act
    (1952), 95
Immigration and Naturalization
    Service (INS), 98
Immigration procedures for refugees,
    60–62
India
  partition of (1947), and religious
    strife, 16
  Tibetan refugees in, 89

Malaysia, 5, 6, 7, 52, 61, 114, 116
Mann, Peggy, 10
Mauritania, 25
McMullen, Maureen, 64, 65
  quoted, 64–65
Medicin Sans Frontieres, 111
Menzious, Merilien, 40
  quoted, 41
Mexico, and Reagan administration,
  103
Miami (Fla.), Cuban refugees in, 39,
  97, 100, 102
Middle East, 73, 96
  turmoil in, 16, 33–34
Mieh Mieh refugee camp (Lebanon),
  72
Mogadishu (Somalia), 66
Monahan, Jim, 67
Mondale, Walter, 114
Mongolian refugees, 97
Morocco, 24
Mozambique, 89
Mussolini, Benito, 13

Nazi concentration camps, 9, 10, 14,
  94
Nepal, 89
Netherlands, 90
  Jewish refugee children in, before
    World War II, 11
  and Nazis, 12
  withdrawal as colonial power of, 18
New York Times, 72, 84, 112
New Zealand, 61
Nguema, Francisco Macias, 25
Nicaragua
  civil war in, 37
  refugees from, 37, 75
Nigeria, Ibos in, 18
Nobel Peace Prize, 106
Nong Hai refugee camp (Thailand),
  57–58

Ogaden region, Ethiopian war in, 21,
  63, 66
Organization of African Unity, 109,
  112, 116

Organization of American States, 109,
  116
Oxfam, 111

Pakistan, 30
  civil war in, 32–33
Palestine, 15, 16, 68
Palestinian refugee problem, 17, 33,
  68–73
Paris (France), refugees in, after World
  War I, 9
Philippines, 82, 114
Phnom Penh (Cambodia), 48, 49, 61
Pogroms in Russia and Poland, 92
Pol Pot regime, 27, 28, 48, 49, 61
Poland
  ethnic Germans in, 42
  immigrants from, in United States,
    92
  invaded by Germany, 12–13
  martial law declared in (1981), 16, 67
  and Nazis, 12
  refugees from (1980s), 21, 67
Prague (Czechoslovakia), refugees in,
  after World War I, 9
Public opinion, role of, 116–118
Pulau Bidong island, refugee camps
  on, 6, 53–55, 60, 62

Quakers (American Friends), 53, 60

Ray, Robert, 83
Reagan, Ronald, 103
Red Cross, 111
"Re-education camps," Vietnamese, 1,
  2, 8, 27
Refugee Act (1980), 97, 98
Refugees (UNHCR publication), 24
Repatriation of refugees, 89, 109
Resettlement of refugees, 77–90
  and special problems of children, 86–
    88
  in United States, 81–85, 88, 110
  in Western nations, 68, 78–80
Rhee, Syngman, 18
Roman Catholic Church, 111
Romans, ancient, 8

Roosevelt, Franklin D., 17–18, 113
Rumania, ethnic Germans in, 42
Russia, 13. *See also* Soviet Union
Russian revolution and civil war
(1917–20), 9

Sa Kaeo refugee camp (Thailand), 29, 47, 55–57, 58
St. Louis, refugees aboard, denied entry into United States, 94
Save the Children Fund, 55, 111
Scandinavia, 111–112
Select Commission on Immigration and Refugee Policy, 100, 102
Shailesh (displaced Asian from Uganda), 88
Singapore, 114
Solidaridád (publication), 37
Solidarity labor union movement, Polish, 16
Solomon (black South African refugee), 44, 45
Somalia, 21, 22, 24, 51, 63, 64, 65, 66, 87, 98, 109
refugee camps in, 64–66, 67, 110
Somoza, Anastasio, 37
South Africa, 25, 44
South America
repressive regimes in, 35
See also Latin America
South Korea, 18, 96
invaded by North Korea (1950), 18
refugees in, from North Korea, 18
South Vietnam, 1, 27
Southeast Asia, 1, 26, 28, 52, 96, 107, 109, 114, 116
Chinese minorities in, 18, 52
refugee camps in, 60, 74, 79
See also Indochina; Vietnam
Soviet Union, 15, 18
Afghanistan invaded by, 30–32
ethnic Germans in, 42
Jews as emigrants from, 67
refugees from, 21, 42, 67
revolution and civil war in (1917–20), 9
Siberian prison camps in, 15

and United States, tensions between, 18, 95
Spain
civil war in, 13
Fascist dictatorship in, 13
Stalin, Joseph, 18
Statue of Liberty, inscription on base of, 93–94
Sudan, 21, 110
Sweden, 90
handicapped refugees resettled in, 85
Switzerland
handicapped refugees resettled in, 78, 85, 86
Tibetan communities in, 89
Syria, Palestinians in, 68

Taylor, Myron C., 113
Thailand, 28, 52, 89, 108, 111
refugee camps in, 46–47, 52, 55–58, 62, 83, 110, 114
Third World, 51, 100, 116
upheavals in, 18–19, 21
Tibet, 89
Timor, East, famine in, 28–30
Tokyo (Japan), 8
Traiskirchen refugee reception center (Austria), 67–68
Truman, Harry, 95
quoted, 95
Turkey, and massacre of Armenians (1916), 9

Uganda, 21, 22
Asians expelled from, 88
UNICEF News, 31
United Nations, 57, 58, 66, 109, 114, 116
refugees defined by, 97
United Nations Children's Fund, 109
United Nations High Commissioner for Refugees (UNHCR), 22, 37, 63, 88, 106, 107, 108, 109, 111, 112, 114, 116
United Nations Relief and Rehabilitation Agency (UNRRA), 15